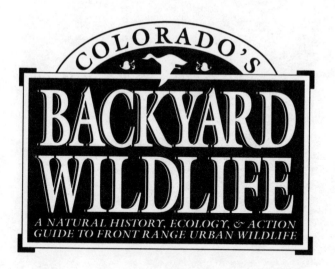

COLORADO'S
BACKYARD
WILDLIFE

A NATURAL HISTORY, ECOLOGY, & ACTION
GUIDE TO FRONT RANGE URBAN WILDLIFE

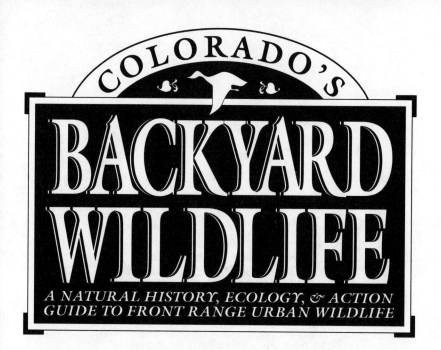

COLORADO'S

BACKYARD
WILDLIFE

A NATURAL HISTORY, ECOLOGY, & ACTION GUIDE TO FRONT RANGE URBAN WILDLIFE

Roberts Rinehart Publishers
A Rhino Book

TEXT AND ILLUSTRATIONS

BY CAROL ANN MOORHEAD

Published by Roberts Rinehart Publishers
Post Office Box 666 Niwot, Colorado 80544
International Standard Book Number 1-879373-08-4
Library of Congress Catalog Card Number 91-67824
Printed in the United States of America

This book was published with the
assistance of the Colorado Division of Wildlife

Cover and book design by Bob Schram, Bookends

CONTENTS

To my dear friend,
Lisa Bryce Lewis

FOREWORD

Colorado's Backyard Wildlife is written for a diverse audience. This audience includes educators and students in grades six and above. It also includes individuals and families. In addition, the book will be useful to leaders and staff members of scouting groups, 4H clubs, nature centers, and camps.

The format of the book was organized with educators in mind, moving from fundamental to more complex ideas as the book progresses. However, if you, your students, or your children are primarily interested in wild urban animals, you may want to move ahead into the ecology and habitat chapters and read the earlier chapters on the benefits of urban wildlife, pest species, and history later.

A teacher's guide developed specifically for this book is available from the Colorado Division of Wildlife. In addition to original activities, it integrates urban wildlife activities from the Project Wild curriculum. The guide targets grades six through nine. Its use in these grades is important because many of the ideas discussed in the book are complex and may require reinforcement through activities and discussion. Educators in other grades and in settings other than the classroom are encouraged to adapt the activities to their own use. To obtain a teacher's guide, please send your request to:

Colorado Division of Wildlife, Project Wild
6060 Broadway, Denver, CO 80216

RESOURCES

For certification of a city or community; residential yard; or school, corporate, or institutional grounds as a wildlife sanctuary/habitat, write:

National Institute for Urban Wildlife
Urban Wildlife Sanctuary Program
10921 Trotting Ridge Way
Columbia, MD 21044

National Wildlife Federation
Backyard Wildlife Habitat Program
1400 16th St. NW
Washington, DC 20036

For information about urban wildlife and related programs in your community, contact:

❖ **Denver**

Colorado Division of Wildlife
Central Region
(303) 297-1192

U.S. Fish and Wildlife Service
Rocky Mountain Arsenal Urban Wildlife Refuge
(303) 289-0132

Denver Museum of Natural History
Education Division
(303) 370-6303 or (303) 370-6371

Denver Audubon Society
Urban Education Project
(303) 757-8376

❖ **Boulder**

Boulder County Parks and Open Space
(303) 441-3950

Boulder City Parks and Recreation
(303) 441-3400

❖ **Fort Collins**

Colorado Division of Wildlife
Northeast Region
(303) 484-2836

City of Fort Collins
Natural Resources Division
(303) 221-6600

Colorado State University Cooperative
Extension
Extension Wildlife and Natural Resources
(303) 491-6411

Northern Colorado Environmental Learning
Center
(303) 491-1661

❖ **Colorado Springs**

Colorado Division of Wildlife
Southeast Region
(719) 473-2945

El Paso County Parks
Bear Creek Nature Center
(719) 520-6387

Colorado Springs Parks and Recreation
Department
Beidleman Environmental Center
(719) 578-7088

❖ **Pueblo**

The Greenway and Nature Center of Pueblo
(719) 545-9114

ACKNOWLEDGEMENTS

I began and almost completed this book during my master's program in the Department of Fishery and Wildlife Biology at Colorado State University. Had I known at the start what I know now, I would have talked myself out of doing it. It was not a sensible master's project, but I wouldn't believe that then. Now, nearly four years after I typed up the outline and thumbnailed the first sketch, the book is ready. Naivety and stubbornness were probably my best friends during the process, but I have many others to thank.

The Colorado Division of Wildlife (CDOW) funded the majority of the work on the book and its teacher's guide. I am indebted to Carol Bylsma, CDOW Environmental Education Coordinator, for seeing the merit of the project and agreeing to support it. I am grateful to Gwendolyn Scott, the educator chosen by CDOW to write the teacher's guide. Her sensitive treatment of the text and her innovative activities greatly enhance the book's educational value. I also appreciate the assistance of the Outdoor Writer's Association of America whose scholarship awards helped support my work in 1988 and 1989.

I thank my graduate committee members, Professor Eugene Decker, Dr. Dale Hein, and Dr. Howard Bruner, for their advice and encouragement during my graduate program and throughout the production of the book. I am especially grateful to Professor Decker, my major advisor, for his unfailing patience while the text grew longer and the illustrations more detailed. I thank him also for reviewing countless drafts of the manuscript.

In addition to my committee members, other knowledgeable individuals reviewed and made comments on the manuscript. I am grateful to Marcene Amends, Dr. Luke George, Jay Thompson, Therese Race Thompson, Elizabeth Webb, and Nancy Zuchlag. I am also thankful for the publisher's copy editors, Julia Tomes and Carrie Jenkins, who caught inconsistencies of format, grammatical glitches, and muddled logic. Other excellent critics were the students of Karen Kristofferson's 1990 sixth grade class at William Lopez Elementary School in Fort Collins and Victoria Anthony's 1990 eighth grade science class at Blevins Junion High School, also in Fort Collins.

A heartfelt thanks goes to my fellow graduate students whose advice, humor, and friendship helped make the process of creating this book possible. I am especially grateful to Cathy Brown, Mari Nakada, Eric Rexstad, Joel Schmutz, Tanya Shenk, Patricia Stevens, Jay Thompson, Therese Race Thompson, and Tracy Wager. I also thank my family for their love and encouragement throughout the project.

My acknowledgements wouldn't be complete without thanking the greatest contributors, the many scientists and naturalists whose work I have drawn upon to write the book. Without them, there would be no theories to discuss, hypotheses to relate, or knowledge about animals to impart. I hope that I have done their work justice. I assume responsibility for any errors that may occur in the text.

Lastly, my deepest gratitude goes to Luke George, my fiance and best friend. He willingly, even cheerfully, put up with countless working weekends so that I could finish this book. I thank him for believing in me and my work.

CHAPTER 1

SOUNDS LIKE A PARTY TO ME!

What exactly is *urban wildlife*? Does a wild Saturday night party come to mind? Or how about those teenagers hanging out on the corner? Or those kids on rollerblades shooting down the street? No, the real meaning of urban wildlife, at least to biologists, is the wild animals and plants that have adjusted to living in city environments.

Colorado's Backyard Wildlife introduces you to a variety of wildlife and habitats that exist along the eastern edge of the Rocky Mountains, a geographic area called the *Front Range*. The Front Range includes a 150-mile strip of urban development extending from Fort Collins to Pueblo, Colorado. About two and a half million people, or four out of every five Coloradans, live in Front Range cities.

Many kinds of urban animals that are commonly seen along the Front Range are discussed in the book, including *species* of birds, mammals, fish, reptiles, amphibians, and spiders. A species is a group of organisms of the same type that can interbreed only with each other (robins and humans are examples of species).

The purpose of *Colorado's Backyard Wildlife* is to increase your knowledge about urban wildlife. It is also to increase your appreciation of the role that habitats play in maintaining wildlife in cities. The book will teach you why some animals can live in cities and why others can not, and what certain species of urban wildlife need to survive. You will also discover why animals behave the way they do, how they interact with their environment, and what you can do to create and protect their *habitat* in your city. The word habitat refers to a species' home or the place where the needs of a species are met. For example, warm-water lakes are the habitat of sunfish. Lastly, you will gain a greater understanding of all wild animals because most of the information in this book also applies to wildlife in natural areas, far away from cities.

While reading, remember that in this book the terms "urban" and "city" refer to big cities as well as to towns and suburbs. Also, the words in italics are ones that may be new to your vocabulary. They are defined both in the text and in the glossary. Finally, you can find all the book's references to certain species and to words in the glossary in the index at the back of the book.

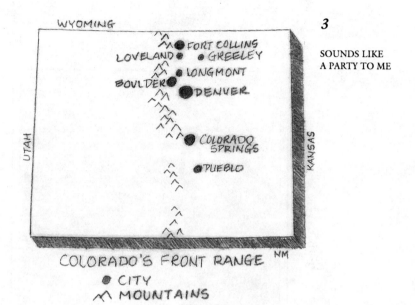

WYOMING

UTAH

KANSAS

FORT COLLINS
LOVELAND • • GREELEY
LONGMONT
BOULDER • • DENVER

COLORADO
SPRINGS
PUEBLO

COLORADO'S FRONT RANGE ᴺᴹ

• CITY
⋀ MOUNTAINS

SOUNDS LIKE
A PARTY TO ME

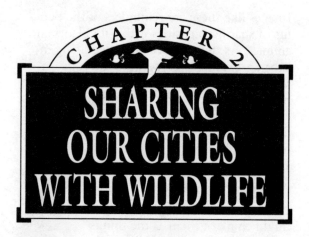

CHAPTER 2

SHARING OUR CITIES WITH WILDLIFE

So, why is urban wildlife so important? Imagine yourself walking to the store and passing not even one tree or bush or patch of grass. Car engines are roaring and people are shouting. Off in the distance is the unnerving racket of a jackhammer. Everywhere you look a blanket of asphalt and concrete smothers the earth, black and gray as far as you can see.

Now picture yourself walking to the store and passing not one but an entire grove of cottonwood trees. The birds are singing in the branches. A squirrel rustles around in the fallen leaves. The earth and plants beneath your feet smell rich and moist, and everything is washed in color. Which route to the store would you rather take?

Images like these are reminders of the benefits of sharing our cities with wild plants and animals. As the number of people living in urban areas increases, so does the concern about creating a healthy and pleasant environment for them. Sociologists, urban ecologists, educators, and others have identified many factors that help make cities desirable places to live. Wild animals are one of those factors. Here are some of the reasons why:

❖ Aesthetic Benefits

Aesthetics are hard to define. You might think of them as the things in life that are beautiful and pleasing. For example, the sad, soft song of a mourning dove and the intricate design of a butterfly's wing have aesthetic value. They capture your imagination and invade your senses. They require you to live in the moment and forget about your worries. Aesthetics remind you that life is rich and diverse and in so doing, they inspire your mind and revive your spirit.

❖ Environmental Benefits

The presence of wild urban animals usually indicates that the environment is healthy for humans as well as wildlife. They are a sign that the city provides quality wildlife habitat—food, water, shelter, and space. Some habitats support a variety of animals, including many *native* species. Native species are those that naturally exist in a particular area, in this case on the eastern edge of the Rocky Mountains. The presence of native species suggests that the natural system with which they evolved is at least partially intact. The fact that natural systems can still function after urbanization shows that they are flexible.

However, they are flexible only to a point. Whether natural systems bend or break under the pressure of urbanization depends on how humans treat them.

Preserving natural areas, conserving natural resources (water, soil, trees, coal, gas, etc.), and polluting as little as possible are ways humans can live in harmony with natural systems. In generous response, these systems provide clean air and water, and fertile soil. Urban animals play essential roles in a functioning natural system. For example, they pollinate plants, disperse seeds, and add nutrients to the soil.

❖ Educational Benefits

Did you know that a chickadee hides thousands of seeds and later, when it is hungry, remembers where to find them? Or that ants create invisible trails by secreting fluids that other ants follow using their antennae? You can observe these and other behaviors right in your backyard or neighborhood park. The behaviors, interactions, and needs of urban wildlife are similar to wildlife in other environments. Thus, learning about the animals you see everyday can also teach you about the animals in those other environments. When you discover an animal that interests you, find out what it is and read about it. Observing and reading are two of the best ways to learn about wildlife.

❖ Economic Benefits

Every year urban wildlife watchers spend millions of dollars on bird seed, binoculars, field guides, nature magazines, and books. Wildlife photographers buy cameras and film. The sale of these items helps store

owners and their employees make a living. In
addition, the city sales tax on each item sold
provides the community with money. This
money is used for schools, buses, road repair,
and other community needs. Thus, directly or
indirectly, all residents benefit from wildlife-
watching activities in their city.

Urban wildlife can also decrease the cost of
maintaining parks, lawns, and gardens. There
is no insecticide that can compete with an
army of insect-eating birds, bats, and garter
snakes. Did you know that one bat can eat
600 to perhaps thousands of insects per hour?
Insect eaters have another advantage over
insecticides—they do not pollute the environment with harmful chemicals.

Higher property values are another economic benefit of urban wildlife. Land with
lots of trees, shrubs, and desirable wildlife
may be as much as 20% more valuable than
land without. Thus, by creating wildlife habitat on your property, you can increase its
value.

❖ **Psychological and Sociological Benefits**

Psychologists have long recognized that people need each other for their happiness and
mental health. More recently, studies have
shown that having a pet can help people feel
less lonely. Perhaps people need contact with

wild plants and animals, too. What do you think?

The joy urban wildlife gives to people is a gift to society. When people are happy, they have energy to work hard, play hard, and give to their family, friends, and community.

❖ Recreational Benefits

Do you like fishing or birdwatching? How about wildlife photography or drawing? If so, you need not go far from home to enjoy these activities. Along the Front Range, there are many places to fish and to watch wildlife. In the Denver area alone, there are nearly two hundred lakes and ponds for fishing. In addition, there are many different places (such as parks, cemeteries, river corridors, lakes, and school yards) where you can watch birds and other animals.

Thousands of city dwellers enjoy wildlife-related activities that people used to think were possible only in wilderness settings. For example, in inner-city Denver you may see peregrine falcons fly and hunt among the skyscrapers. The Colorado Division of Wildlife, as a part of their Watchable Wildlife program, has created areas near cities where you can view wildlife. At the Rocky Mountain Arsenal, just north of Denver, you can observe mule deer, bald eagles, coyotes, prairie dogs, many species of hawks, and other animals in their natural setting. In addition, many nature centers and conservation organizations offer guided bird walks and nature hikes in Front Range cities.

Coyote

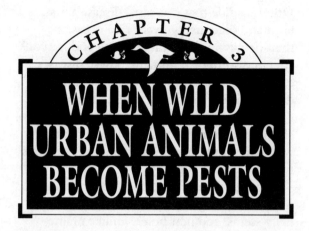

CHAPTER 3

WHEN WILD URBAN ANIMALS BECOME PESTS

*A*lthough urban wildlife is usually desirable, there are times when wild urban animals become *pests*. Pests are those animals that spread disease, raid gardens, destroy or deface property, or for other reasons cause problems for humans.

Some of the typical wildlife pests are raccoons, skunks, bats, pigeons, starlings, pocket gophers, and flickers.

Raccoons, skunks, and bats can carry *rabies*, a serious disease that is transmissible to humans. However, the chance of contracting rabies is extremely rare. The last documented case of rabies in Colorado was in 1927 and was transmitted by a dog bite.

Other wildlife that can carry disease are starlings and pigeons. On very rare occasions their droppings have caused lung and nervous system disorders in humans. These diseases can be transmitted to humans by airborne dust particles from dried starling and pigeon droppings. Contracting these diseases, although extremely unlikely, is one reason why you should prevent pigeons and starlings from nesting in your attic.

Other problems more commonly associated with wildlife pests are burrow entrances, tunnel systems, and nest holes. Unlike prairie dogs, pocket gophers have adjusted to the lush, grassy lawns of Front Range cities. To the dismay of many, they sometimes dig burrows in backyards, gardens, and parks. Pocket gophers spend most of their lives underground in extensive tunnel systems, some of which may be as long as 500 feet. There they feed on roots and vegetation that they pull down from the surface. On rare occasions, they come above ground to eat grasses and other plants.

Pocket Gopher

A sure sign of pocket gophers are the mounds of loose dirt that cover the entrance holes to their burrows.

To most people, seeing a flicker near their home is a delight. However, to those with cedar shingles or siding on their houses, flickers are a dreaded sight. During the spring and early summer, flickers look for nest sites. Although most make their nest cavities in trees, others won't hesitate to make your cedar house their home. They may simply peck the cedar siding in search of insects or actually hammer a nest hole right into the side of the house. Some just like to make noise to attract a mate or to let other flickers know where their home is.

In Colorado, beavers, Canada geese, and mule deer have also been labeled as pests. In certain areas of Denver, beavers have cut down trees in public parks and on private property. In addition, some of Denver's beaver have been known to carry a bacterial disease that can be transmitted to pets and humans.

To many persons in Fort Collins and other Front Range cities, the sight and sounds of Canada geese evoke a mixture of emotions. Although a pleasure to see and hear, Canada geese can be pests. In addition to the many migrating geese that now spend the winter in Fort Collins, there is a large year-round population. These birds leave lots of droppings on golf courses, yards, and public parks.

Boulder residents have conflicting feelings about mule deer. In the warmer months they enjoy seeing the abundance of deer in the nearby foothills. However, when winter arrives and the deer head for the lowlands, many residents object to having them in their backyards and parks. Mule deer eat valuable trees and shrubs and they raid gardens in springtime. Sometimes they interfere with traffic. In addition, many persons fear that the high numbers of deer are attracting predatory mountain lions to the area. The abundance of deer is due, in part, to the open space lands on the outskirts of the city. This land provides plentiful food, water, and space, as well as protection from hunters.

Canada Goose

Wildlife pest management is a growing discipline, the details of which are beyond the scope of this book. If you have questions or need solutions to specific problems contact the Colorado Division of Wildlife, or the Colorado State University Cooperative Extension office in your county. In addition, city parks and recreation offices, animal control offices, and nature centers may be able to offer some help.

For city residents to enjoy the benefits of urban wildlife they must develop a reasonable tolerance for most wildlife activities. Urban planners and wildlife managers try to control the conflicts that arise between wildlife and humans whenever possible. However, meeting both the needs of wildlife and the desires of humans is difficult. After reading this book, perhaps you will agree that the pleasures of sharing your city with and living close to wild animals far outweigh most of the problems.

*House
Sparrows*

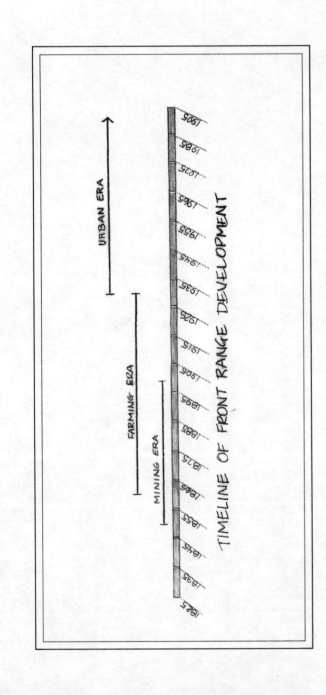

TIMELINE OF FRONT RANGE DEVELOPMENT

CHAPTER 4

THE HISTORY OF COLORADO'S FRONT RANGE

*H*ow strange and frightening it must have been for Native Americans as the first settlements of non-native people sprang up along the Front Range, lands that they had inhabited alone for thousands of years. Or how elated Fort Collins farmers must have felt when water first flowed onto their croplands from their newly built irrigation lines. Or how dramatically different lifestyles became for Coloradans after the advent of the automobile and then again, after the construction of Interstates 25 and 70. Looking back and considering the past helps puts life as it is today in perspective. If studied carefully, the past can help put the future in order.

Since settlers of European descent arrived on the Front Range in the 1800s, the landscape and the lifestyles of the people have changed notably decade after decade, and recently, year after year. These changes in landscape and lifestyle have happened because people made certain decisions and took certain actions. In other words, your environment is a consequence of the decisions and actions made by people who came before you. This is important to realize because it means that what you decide and how you act determine how people in the future will live. Needless to say, determining other peoples' futures is a big responsibility.

In just over 130 years the Front Range has changed from a grassland into an agricultural environment and then into an urban environment. Although most of Colorado's land is wild or rural, the Front Range has only traces of its wilderness and agricultural past.

The shift in land use has influenced the *settlement patterns* and the number of people living along the Front Range. As you might imagine, these changes have affected the area's wildlife. Below is a historical description of the Front Range and the changes that occurred during the mining, farming, and urban eras.

1825

❖ MINING ERA *(1850-1900)*

The first population boom in Colorado occurred after miners struck gold in the late 1850s and again in the 1890s. As a result, towns like Denver and Colorado City (now a part of Colorado Springs) sprang up to provide for the miners' needs with food, goods, and services. Eventually, Denver became a manufacturing center for mining machinery and Pueblo grew into one of the largest steel manufacturing cities in the west.

Effects on Wildlife and Habitats. Miners and residents of mining and supply towns caused a serious decline in local elk and deer *populations* by their excessive hunting. Populations are groups of individuals of a particular species. There were no restrictions on how many animals hunters could take, nor when they could hunt.

Small-scale habitat destruction occurred at the sites of mines, mining towns, and supply centers. As a result, there probably were additional but minor declines in wildlife populations. Chemicals leached out from some old mines and contaminated nearby streams, groundwater, and soil. The presence of these chemicals determined which plants and animals can live in the area today.

1925

❖ FARMING ERA
(Approximately 1860-1930)

During the mining era, some settlers decided that growing food for the miners was more lucrative than mining, so they bought land and became farmers. The most successful farms were ones that belonged to *farm colonies*. These colonies were planned communities where members paid dues and worked together to build irrigation systems. Wise planning and plenty of irrigation water were the keys to success. Greeley, Longmont, and Fort Collins began as colony towns.

By 1900, the mining boom was over and farming had become the main industry along the Front Range. During the farming era, population growth was gradual and the people were thinly spread across the land.

Effects on Wildlife and Habitats. The greatest impact to wildlife during the farming era was the loss of habitat as farmers turned *prairie,* or grassland, into agricultural fields. Lands bordering rivers were farmed first because of their fertile soils. These areas were also valuable habitat because they supported a variety and abundance of wildlife.

Loss of habitat caused a reduction in animal numbers. However, acres of grassland still remained between farms, and strips of prairie existed between agricultural fields. These areas provided enough habitat to ensure the survival of many of the native wildlife species.

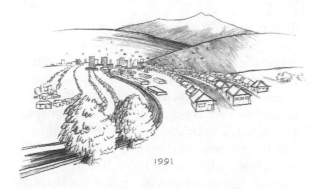

1991

❖ URBAN ERA *(1930-present)*

The year 1930 marked the beginning of Colorado's urban era because it was the first year that more people lived in cities than in the country. During this and the following years, severe drought and economic depression forced many farmers to give up their land and move to cities. Urban growth was slow during the Depression and the U.S. involvement in World War II (1941-1945). However, highways, railways, and an airport were built during this time. They set the stage for rapid urban growth after the war.

The state's economy improved as businesses that depended on interstate highways and air travel moved to Colorado. Further economic development occurred as federal government agencies and energy companies established their headquarters in the state.

Today, tourism and outdoor recreation are growing industries in Colorado. Each year more and more people visit the state to sightsee, camp, hike, hunt, fish, and ski. As more jobs are created, many of the people who initially came for the sun, scenery, and snow come back to work and live in Front Range cities.

Effects on Wildlife and Habitats. The widespread conversion of farmland and natural areas into urban developments has resulted in extensive loss of native wildlife habitat. Some native species have not been able to adjust to urban conditions, while others have prospered. The creation of *non-native* habitats in cities has attracted many non-native species of wildlife to the Front Range. (Nonnative refers to habitats or species that do not naturally exist in their present location.)

The effects of urbanization on wildlife and habitats are both profound and interesting. The remainder of this book explores these effects, the role of ecology in understanding them, and the interactions among animals and plants in some of the most common city habitats.

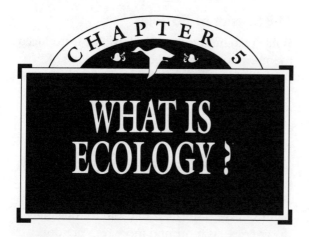

CHAPTER 5

WHAT IS ECOLOGY ?

*T*his book is about the *natural history* and *ecology* of Front Range urban wildlife. Sometimes the terms natural history and ecology are used interchangeably, but there is a subtle difference between the two. Natural history is the non-scientific study of animal and plant life and the natural environment, usually of a particular region. You can learn a lot about natural history by reading scientific literature and nature magazines, taking natural science courses, and observing animals and plants in the field. Ecology, on the other hand, is the scientific study of how living things interact with each other and their environment. Some people think that this discipline is restricted to wilderness areas far from cities, but that's simply not true. Ecological interactions take place and can be studied scientifically in all environments, including suburbs and cities.

While reading this book, you will be introduced to important ecological concepts. Many of these ideas were first tested by ecologists working in areas far away from cities. However, most have been found to be tried and true in cities, as well. "Tried and true" ideas are called *theories.*

Compared to chemistry and physics, ecology is a young science and has many new theories. Because there is still so much to learn about nature, there is still a lot of room for making discoveries. As more and more tests are done, old ecological ideas and even theories will be replaced by new ones. One day some of the ideas in this book will seem old and outdated, but that's alright. You can be sure that they will give rise to new ideas and perhaps better answers.

Ecologists, like all scientists, ask questions about what they see. For example, a behavioral ecologist once wondered how barn owls locate their prey. He asked himself if it is by sight, smell, sound, or by feeling heat from the prey's body. Because the ecologist was really interested in knowing the answer, he formulated a *hypothesis.* A hypothesis is a possible explanation of a behavior or trait. His hypothesis may have been that barn owls find their prey by sound—by hearing the prey move or make noises. The ecologist probably made some predictions, one of which may have been that barn owls would be able to catch mice even if they couldn't see or smell them, or feel the warmth from their bodies. Next he designed an experiment that could test the predictions and either support or fail to support the hypothesis. The ecologist put a barn owl in a totally dark room with a mouse. To test whether the owl was lead to the mouse by its sound, odor, or warmth, he attached a piece of paper to a thread which he then tied to the mouse's hind leg. Time after time in total darkness, this barn owl and others landed on the rustling piece of paper, not the mouse. The results of the experiment supported his hypothesis that barn owls located prey by sound.

This process of asking questions, formulating hypotheses, and making and testing predictions is called the *scientific method*. Many people find science exciting because by using the scientific method they have the opportunity to expand society's knowledge about the world. For example, you now know that the most current scientific research indicates that barn owls locate prey by sound.

As you read the following chapters and look at the habitat pictures, questions about nature and the way it works may pop into your head. No matter how simple your questions may seem, don't dismiss them. If you feel inclined, make some predictions of your own, and maybe even design your own experiment. Just thinking about and discussing the possible answers will teach you a lot about the science of ecology.

❖ Interdependence

One concept that ecological studies support again and again is the *interdependence* of living and non-living "elements." Interdependence means that each element is somewhat, if not totally, dependent on the other for its ability to function. To grasp the concept of interdependence it may help to think of the components of *ecosystems.*

Ecosystems are groups of living and non-living things that function together in a particular environment. For example, prairie dogs, birds, many insects, low-lying grasses, and shrubs (living elements) interact with each other as well as with dry soil, high winds, and occasional downpours (non-living elements) to make up the shortgrass prairie ecosystem.

The elements of a *community* are interdependent, too. All the organisms that live together in an ecosystem comprise a community. In the above example, prairie dogs, birds, insects, grasses, and shrubs make up the shortgrass prairie community. It is possible to find interdependencies or draw connections among all elements of ecosystems and communities. Some of the connections are closer than others. For example, it is easy to understand a bird's dependence on insects, but harder to visualize soil's connection to prairie dogs. By burrowing, though, prairie dogs actually loosen and aerate the soil, making it possible for water to seep in deeper and for plant roots to get established. In turn, moisture and plant cover protect prairie

ECOSYSTEMS:

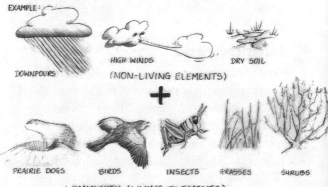

EXAMPLE:

DOWNPOURS   HIGH WINDS   DRY SOIL

(NON-LIVING ELEMENTS)

+

PRAIRIE DOGS   BIRDS   INSECTS   GRASSES   SHRUBS

COMMUNITY (LIVING ELEMENTS)

soils from wind *erosion*. Erosion means the
gradual wearing away of land surface by wind,
water, ice, or other natural forces.

Although ecosystems and communities are
usually portrayed as natural areas, urban ecosystems and communities are just as valid. Try to
find the interdependence among humans,
domestic cats, songbirds, shade trees, golf
courses, buildings, and roads.

❖ The Importance of Habitat

Another important ecological concept is that
habitat is the key to every animal's survival,
including your own. Good habitat has four
essential components—food, water, shelter, and
space. Each species has different requirements
for the types and amounts of each *habitat component*. These requirements vary from season to
season. Habitat components must be of high
quality, in the proper amounts, and within reasonable traveling distance of each other to be of
ultimate benefit to an animal. All animals
require the four essential habitat components—
whether they live on the plains, in the mountains, or in the city. You may want to consider
what components make up your habitat.

In the following chapters you will learn
about five common urban habitats and some of
the species that live in each. The habitats are
the urban edge, the inner city, the backyard (in
summer and winter), the riparian corridor (in
spring) and the park and open space (in fall).
Over sixty species of urban wildlife are discussed and almost all are illustrated. However,
these habitats and species are by no means the
only ones on the Front Range. There are
countless habitat types and over 350 common
species of wildlife that exist in this area.

CHAPTER 6

URBAN EDGE AND INNER CITY HABITATS

*B*efore reading this chapter, turn back a page and spend a few minutes looking at the illustration. Compare the two habitats and develop some of your own ideas about the potential effects of urbanization on wildlife. How do the habitats differ? How are they similar? What differences do you notice about the species in each habitat?

The preceding illustration shows two habitats in Colorado's urban ecosystem: on the left is the urban edge habitat and on the right is the inner-city habitat. These are two of the most extreme habitats associated with cities. The urban ecosystem is made up of many habitat types. Each habitat has characteristic plants and animals. Together these species make up the urban community. As you can see in this illustration, the *composition*, or make-up, of the community changes dramatically between the urban edge and inner-city habitats.

By comparing and contrasting the species in the two habitats illustrated, you can see some of the effects that urbanization has on wildlife communities. In the urban edge habitat depicted here, the urban and the grassland ecosystems overlap. Except for the disturbance from nearby suburbs, this habitat is similar to parts of the grassland ecosystem. Consequently, all of the species are native to the grasslands of eastern Colorado. On the other hand, most of the species in the illustrated inner city habitat are not native to the Front Range area. Why is this so?

❖ **Generalists and Specialists**

Life in the inner city is much different from life in the country or even in the suburbs. There are many opportunities for survival, but only for those species that can adjust. These species tend to be *generalists*, those whose survival needs are not specific and who can change their behavior to take advantage of new opportunities.

Not many native grassland animals are generalists. In fact, most of the animals in the urban edge habitat are grassland *specialists*, species whose survival needs are specific to the grasslands. These animals have evolved with each other and with the grasslands for thousands of years. As a result, they are specially adapted to living in the dry grasslands where it is hot in summer and cold in winter. Many of them can not adjust to highly-developed urban environments.

❖ Specialists of the Grasslands

Prairie dogs are an example of a specialist. They require large tracts of open land for their colonies or "towns" and unobstructed views for seeing predators at a distance. A crowded inner city can not provide either of these requirements. However, if given enough open space, prairie dogs can coexist with humans in less-developed urban areas.

Prairie dogs dig tunnels and burrows in the arid prairie soil. This digging behavior is an *adaptation* to life on the prairie. Adaptations are behaviors or traits that help an organism survive in its environment. They result from an animal (or plant) interacting with its environment for a long time, often thousands or millions of years. Burrows provide prairie dogs with cool retreats in summer and snug shelters in winter, as well as protection from predators and the occasional grassland fire. Even the burrow entrance mounds are constructed in a way that increases air flow through the tunnels. It's no wonder that rattlesnakes, burrowing owls, and rabbits take shelter in prairie dog burrows, too.

Prairie Dog

Prairie dogs are active grounds-keepers. They clip vegetation around their mounds, graze the prairie grasses, and dig up the soil while looking for roots to eat. Over time, these activities change the plant community of their towns from mostly grasses to mostly *forbs* (leafy, non-woody plants). If the prairie dog town in this illustration were not so close to the suburbs, the abundance of forbs would probably attract the shy pronghorn antelope. As it is, the altered community does attract western meadowlarks and lark buntings, which have an easier time finding insects and seeds in the thin plant cover.

Aside from the beautiful meadowlark, the male lark bunting may be the most striking songbird of the prairie. The breeding *plumage*, or covering of feathers, of the male is dramatically different from its brown-streaked plumage of winter. In June, they arrive on the grasslands sporting a lustrous black coat with bright white wing patches. After setting up their small territories, the males begin their courtship displays. They fly straight up into the air, unfold their wings, burst into song and then drop slowly, like a falling leaf, to the ground. Ecologists think that these aerial displays are an adaptation to the treeless plains. They believe that to a female, the male is as impressive and eye-catching singing in the air as he would be from the top of a tree. Apparently they caught the eye of public school students in Denver—they chose the lark bunting as Colorado's state bird.

Big city life suits neither meadowlarks nor lark buntings. Like many other

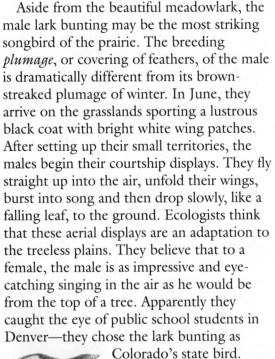

*Western
Meadowlark*

Lark Bunting

grassland birds, these birds nest on the ground. Can you imagine how long their eggs would last if they nested on a city sidewalk?

The loggerhead shrike is a common but rarely seen bird of the prairie. Shrikes nest in bushes or on the low limbs of the occasional small tree. They are sometimes called "butcher birds" because of a very unusual behavior. Shrikes impale insects, small rodents, snakes, and birds on thorns of trees or the barbs of barbed wire fences (note the grasshopper). There are various theories to explain this behavior.

*Loggerhead
Shrike*

One theory is that the use of thorns is an adaptation for having small feet. Unlike most birds of prey, shrikes' feet are not strong enough for securing larger prey items while they rip and tear them with their beaks. Another theory is that shrikes store food on barbs and thorns for use in the cold months of winter. Still another theory is that male shrikes impale their prey for display and warning purposes. A well-stocked pantry might attract a female or inform another male of an already occupied territory. Of course, it is possible that the behavior of impaling can be explained by a combination of these theories.

Shrikes hunt from perches. Before barbed-wire fences and telephone lines, the only grassland perches available were stalks of yucca plants, bushes, and occasionally a small tree. What effect, if any, do you think that human-built perches and barbs have had on the numbers of shrikes? Are shrikes more successful at hunting prey from natural or human-built perches? These are the types of questions that ecologists ask themselves and attempt to answer through ecological studies.

URBAN EDGE
AND INNER CITY
HABITATS

38 Adjusting to City Life

Unlike the loggerhead shrike, the American
kestrel (a small falcon) has shown an ability to
adjust to city life. However, city kestrels adopt
a slightly different lifestyle from country
kestrels. For example, instead of nesting on
rock ledges or in tree holes, city kestrels nest
on telephone poles, roof gutters, and the
ledges of buildings.

The diets of city and country kestrels also differ. Kestrels are *raptors*, birds that kill their prey.
Other examples of raptors, or birds of prey, are
hawks, owls, and eagles. In the illustration of
the urban edge habitat, kestrels would eat
insects and small mammals, such as white-footed mice. On occasion they might even eat small
bullsnakes. However, in the inner city habitat
they would order from a different menu, one
with European starlings, pigeons, house sparrows, and perhaps a house mouse or Norway
rat. One starling or two sparrows easily satisfies
a kestrel's daily requirements.

City kestrels differ from country kestrels in
other ways, too. For example, city kestrels
usually do not migrate south for the winter.
Cities are typically warmer than the surrounding countryside during winter. Also, abundant small birds provide a ready source of
food throughout the year. City kestrels (and
other urban birds) often nest earlier and lay
more eggs than those living in the country.
This may also be due to the milder climates
and year-round food supplies of cities.

Higher average temperatures have earned
cities the name of *heat islands*. There are
many reasons why cities are warmer than their
surrounding environments. Heat from

schools and houses and especially from industrial sources is released into the air around cities. Another reason is that city skyscrapers often obstruct air flow and as a result can diminish the cooling effect of circulating air. (Skyscrapers have also been known to act as wind tunnels, which have the opposite effect.) In addition, buildings heat up more during the day and cool off less at night than water, grass, and other vegetation. Lastly, high levels of pollutants in the air trap heat and prevent it from dissipating into the atmosphere. Higher temperatures in cities, in turn, significantly influence other environmental conditions. For example, when temperatures climb, moisture levels decline, and soils become drier. These environmental changes affect the plant and animal community, sometimes causing the species composition to change.

Another urban edge species that has adapted to the urban environment is the bullsnake. However, it is more likely to be found in the lesser-developed suburbs than in the inner city. Bullsnakes are well-adapted to the grasslands where they feed on insects, white-footed mice, and the eggs of ground-nesting birds like the meadowlark.

White-footed mice and monarch butterflies are as much at home in the city as they are on the prairie. The mice feed on the abundant seeds of prairie plants as well as on grain crops (note the ear of corn in the habitat picture). They reproduce rapidly and in great numbers. Consequently, white-footed mice are a ready source of food for predators both inside and outside of city limits.

During the summer, monarch butterflies can be found

Bullsnake

40

URBAN EDGE
AND INNER CITY
HABITATS

almost anywhere milkweed plants grow (note the pink flower in the picture). Without milkweeds, monarchs could not survive. They drink the plant's nectar and lay their eggs on the leaves. When the eggs hatch, the *larvae,* the young stage of an insect's life, eat the leaves. Not only do the plants provide the butterflies with food, they also give them their best defense. Milkweeds produce potent chemicals that most animals avoid. However, monarchs use them to their advantage. By eating the toxic leaves, monarchs themselves become bad-tasting to would-be predators. As a result, a predator's first monarch is usually its last.

❖ Inner City Residents

Colorado has little inner city habitat compared to some states. Along the Front Range, there is an abundance of land and few *zoning laws,* laws that control where and what you can build. As a result, there is scattered, outward growth instead of crowded, upward growth typical of many cities. However, Denver does have a crowded downtown and many Front Range communities have congested areas with at least some inner-city conditions.

As mentioned earlier, none of the species in the inner-city habitat illustration is native to Colorado. In fact, most of them

Starling

are native to Europe and have taken up residence in cities throughout the world. Their ability to colonize areas over such a broad geographic range indicates that these species are generalists.

You may be wondering how species from Europe ended up living in Colorado. Unlike most people who immigrate to the United States, starlings, house sparrows, pigeons, and Norway rats did not make a conscious effort to move here. They were brought here either intentionally by well-meaning people (starlings, house sparrows, and pigeons) or unintentionally on boats (Norway rats). Starlings and house sparrows can teach us an important lesson about the problems of introducing *exotics* (non-native species) into new places.

Both starlings and house sparrows were brought from England to the United States in the mid to late 1800s. Starlings were introduced into New York City's Central Park by a man who wanted to pay tribute to the playwright William Shakespeare. His goal was to have all the birds mentioned in Shakespeare's plays living in the park. Little did he know that in less than one hundred years, city dwellers, farmers, and naturalists all across North America would consider his prized bird a major pest.

Another well-intentioned person introduced house sparrows into New York as early as 1850. He wanted them as reminders of his European homeland. Others hoped that the house sparrows would control an outbreak of the snow-white linden moth, the larvae of which were eating the leaves off the trees. Like starlings, house sparrows spread rapidly

House Sparrow

across the United States, raiding grain crops and competing for nest holes with native birds. In cities they flourished, building nests in every conceivable place (note the lamp post) and defiling property with their droppings.

❖ Ecological Niches

Norway rats and pigeons, also immigrants from Europe, have a similar story of rapid population growth and expansion across the United States. These generalists were success-ful because they were able to fill *ecological niches* in the city. Niches are more than just places where animals of a particular species are found; they are the roles that animals play in an ecosystem. For example, the mead-owlark plays the role of a daytime, insect-eat-ing, ground-nesting bird of the grasslands. The meadowlark's position within the habitat (on the ground or a low perch), its activities (feeding, building, nesting, etc.), and the time of day of its activities are all factors that make up the meadowlark's or any animal's niche. Other ecological niches of the grass-land are burrow-digging, root-eaters (prairie dogs); tree-nesting, high-perching predators (kestrels); and airborne nectar-drinkers (monarch butterflies). How would you describe your ecological niche?

Compared to grassland species, the roles of inner-city species are less specific. Perhaps this is because inner-cities are relatively new habitats and the species are gen-eralists instead of specialists. Nonetheless, inner-city species have created their niches. For example, city pigeons are

Pigeon

garbage-eating ledge-dwellers. They eat sprin-
kled bread crumbs, littered leftovers (note the
french fries), insects, and seeds and berries
from urban plants. Their roost and nest sites
are the ledges, sills, nooks, and crannies of
downtown buildings. These sites are not too
different from the rocky cliffs of Europe,
Africa, and Asia where they originated.

Starlings are more particular about their
nest sites than pigeons. They choose holes
that are one to one and a half inches wide and
ten to thirty feet above the ground. Their diet
is similar to the pigeon's, except that they eat
more insects. Starlings' bodies are built for
digging insects out of the soil. A common
sight in parks or on lawns is a flock of starlings walking (not hopping as most birds do)
across the grass. They have large, strong legs
for walking and sturdy beaks for digging up
insects. However, in the inner city, starlings
are more likely to find their prey at garbage
cans, where insects are attracted to rotting
food and sugary soft drink cans. When fall
arrives, starlings will add seeds and fruit to
their diet if any are available. They even have
been known to eat dog food!

House sparrows, which are actually weaver-
birds and not sparrows at all, weave their
nests almost anywhere. These coarse structures, which have a front door, are constructed in roof gutters, lamp posts, ledges, holes,
and mailboxes. House sparrows also dine on
insects at garbage cans. They are fond of
seeds, especially of such plant pests as dande-
lions, ragweed, and crab grass. Although
pigeons, starlings, and house sparrows can
cause problems for city dwellers with their

Norway Rat

excessive noise and defacing of property, they also are valuable in reducing the numbers of plant and insect pests.

Unlike pigeons, starlings, and house sparrows, it is hard to find the redeeming qualities of Norway rats. These urban residents spend most of their time underground in the crawl spaces and basements of buildings. They use sewer pipes as mock subways, swimming to and fro beneath the city streets. At night they may come above ground to look for food, particularly around garbage cans.

❖ Conclusion

Colorado's urban ecosystem is a patchwork of habitats. The patches are diverse, ranging from the urban edge at one extreme to the inner city at the other. In the next four chapters, you will learn about other urban habitats. Each habitat has been urbanized to a different degree. Compare and contrast the different habitats and the numbers and kinds of species that live in each. Try forming your own opinion about what degree and type of urban development benefits wildlife and humans the most.

Pigeons

carol ann muorhead '91

CHAPTER 7

BACKYARD HABITAT IN THE SUMMER

*U*rban backyards are seldom natural. Like the inner city they are human creations. The difference, of course, is in the components. Instead of concrete slabs and steel beams, backyards are made of trees, shrubs, and lawn grasses. However, despite these living parts, most backyard habitat in urban Colorado is entirely different from the native habitats of the Front Range.

Raccoon

Habitat Alteration Affects Community Composition

As discussed in the chapter on the history of Colorado's Front Range, chapter four, urbanization alters native habitat. In turn, habitat alteration affects the composition of wildlife communities. It does so either by displacing native species, or by creating habitats to which some natives and non-natives can adjust. The wildlife community in the summer backyard scene demonstrates the various outcomes of habitat alteration.

For example, this backyard may once have been part of a prairie dog town, though prairie dogs could not live here now. Exotic lawn grass has replaced the native prairie grasses on which they depend. In addition, the fenced-in area is not large enough for a prairie dog town. Nor is it open enough to provide unobstructed views of approaching predators. This habitat no longer provides the *resources* that prairie dogs need, and as specialists, prairie dogs can not adapt to this changed environment. Resources are components of the environment that are used by plants and animals including humans.

On the other hand, the native raccoon has found abundant resources in this backyard.

Raccoons have adjusted well to urban condi-

tions. Some studies show that there are more
raccoons in urban areas than in rural areas.
This is in part due to the abundance of waste-
food in urban areas (note the open garbage
can). Urban raccoons eat just about anything:
birdseed, dog food, garbage, dormant insects,
and fruit and vegetables from the garden. But
raccoons are hard to catch in the act because
they rest during the day and are *nocturnal*, or
active at night.

Another Front Range native that thrives in
urban environments is the eastern cottontail.
Unlike prairie dogs, cottontails eat exotic
grasses. They also prefer areas with tall vegetation. Trees and shrubs provide shade and safe
places to hide from predators, just like the
brushy areas and dense grasses of its native
habitat.

Despite the abundance of protective vegetation in cities, urban cottontails are the preferred targets for many predators, such as cats,
dogs, hawks, and owls. The cottontail's best
defense is its ability to escape. In fact, if you
study its body carefully you will see that it is
well-adapted for detecting predators and for
fast get-aways. For example, the eyes are set
high on its head, which helps the rabbit see
would-be predators even when its head is low-
ered. It also has big ears with which to detect
sounds from far away. When it does sense dan-
ger, its strong hind legs propel it to   *Cottontail*
safety. A cottontail's behav-
ior makes escape easier.
For example, it stays close
to tall grass and bushes,
where it can quickly hide
if danger arises.

Cottontail populations can withstand the abundance of predators because they have high reproductive rates. They breed throughout the warmer months and have several litters in a season, usually two to six young per litter. The *kits*, or baby rabbits, are born in shallow holes, which mothers line with grasses, forbs, and soft fur plucked from their undersides.

Another common backyard breeder in Colorado is the American robin. Robins are so common in Front Range cities that you might be surprised to learn that they did not always live in the grasslands of eastern Colorado.

American Robins

Although robins are not native to the arid grasslands, they are native to the wooded river bottoms of the Front Range, as well as to the foothills and mountains.

❖ Limiting Factors

Before the urban era, *limiting factors* prevented robins from colonizing much of the Front Range. A limiting factor is a habitat requirement that is in short supply. It limits a population's ability to grow, stay healthy, or even survive in a particular area. For example, before urbanization of the arid Front Range, trees and food were limiting factors for robins. There were not many low-limbed trees for building nests, and not enough insect larvae and worms in the upper layers of soil to sustain a robin population.

Today, the conditions for robins are much different. The lush, shaded lawns of Front Range cities provide them with ideal habitat. Looking in this backyard you see a

Domestic Cat

cottonwood with a low limb on which the
robin can build its nest of grass and mud.
Because of regular watering, insect larvae and
worms live just under the soil's surface, within
reach of a robin's probing beak. There is also
plenty of shade and water for drinking and
bathing. Lastly, there are many bushes where
robins can hide from predators and eat berries
in the fall.

During summer, robins spend most of their
time pulling worms and insect larvae out of the
ground to feed themselves and their young. As
ground-feeders, they are especially vulnerable
to predators. In cities, domestic cats (and perhaps cars) are the robin's most threatening
predators. One study even suggests that cats
are the primary reason that twice as many
robins die in urban areas as in rural areas.

*Tiger
Swallowtail*

❖ Backyard Residents

Another species that benefits from the lush
grass of urban backyards is the native plains
garter snake. Its natural habitat on the *plains,*
or flat, treeless country, is the shores and shallow waters of ponds, lakes, and streams. In
general, garter snakes are active both day and
night during summer months. However, on
especially hot days, they will cool themselves in
a pool of water and rest in the shadows of a
rock pile.

Tiger swallowtails are also at home in backyard habitat. These native butterflies sip nectar
from the flowers of cottonwoods, willows,
aspens, and other native trees and shrubs. They
also like the juices of *carrion,* the rotting flesh
of a dead animal. The one in this picture is
male. He is patrolling the shady backyard,
looking for a female with whom he can mate.

Brown Creeper

54

SUMMER
BACKYARD
HABITAT

If he finds one, a courtship dance will likely follow. Together they will fly up into the air and flutter around each other for a few minutes. Afterwards they will land and mate.

Looking especially bright against the green leaves of summer is the yellow warbler. These insect eaters are native to the Front Range and often spend their summers in the shrubbery of yards or along river banks. They build their nests in the forked branches of small trees or bushes. Yellow warbler nests look like tiny cups. They are made of fine grasses, fur, and lichens bound together with spider silk or the webbing of caterpillar nests.

Another native backyard bird is the brown creeper. These small, well-camouflaged birds spend most of their time on the trunks of big, old trees. Living up to their name, they appear to creep over the bark's surface as they spiral up the trunk. They probe the nooks and crannies in search of adult insects, as well as insect eggs and larvae. Once near the top of the tree, they fly down to the base of the next tree and start all over again.

One of the most showy and aggressive birds of the urban backyard is the blue jay. They are fascinating birds, perhaps even smart. They can mimic the songs and calls of black-capped chickadees, orioles, and other songbirds, as well as the high-pitched scream of hawks. In the fall blue jays *cache,* or store in a hidden place, seeds and nuts. During the winter and spring when they are hungry they remember where to find them.

Pairs of blue jays often stay together for several years. During the nesting season these pairs remain separate from other blue jays. However, in late summer or early fall they band together in family groups or small flocks. Biologists have noted interesting social behavior among the members of these flocks. In one case, a biologist observed younger jays feeding, guarding, and leading to water an older, handicapped jay.

❖ Range Expansion

Blue jays, which appear completely at home in our yards, are actually relatively recent arrivals to Colorado. They began to appear in various places along the Front Range in the 1970s and 1980s. Blue jays are native to forests of the eastern United States. They extended their range westward as forested habitat was created across the Great Plains.

These new "forests" of the Great Plains were actually nothing more than residential yards planted with non-native hardwood trees, and river corridors lined with cottonwoods and other native trees. Both forest types resulted from increased human population growth in the Great Plains states. Planting backyards with shade trees, shrubbery, and lush grasses was (and still is) an attempt to make hot areas like the Great Plains more hospitable. For many who originated from the east coast, it may also have been an effort to re-create a familiar forested environment.

The growth of native trees on rivers that span the Great Plains was a natural consequence of water diversion for irrigation and dam building. As more irrigation canals and dams were built, there

Blue Jay

56

SUMMER
BACKYARD
HABITAT

was more control of flood-
waters. As a result, there were
fewer intense floods to scour the
river banks and sweep away young
trees. Cottonwoods, willows, and other trees
began to flourish. Like stepping stones, forested river banks and urban backyards gave blue
jays a way to cross the otherwise treeless Great
Plains.

Only a generalist like the blue jay could
adapt so readily to new habitats. In fact, the
native scrub jay, a relative of the blue jay, could
not begin to make a living in the backyard
illustrated here. Scrub jays are specialists and
require habitat with native pinon, juniper, and
scrub oak trees. Therefore the establishment of
lush backyards, which creates habitat for blue
jays, has the potential to destroy habitat for
their native relatives. Cases like this, in which
human desires come into conflict with species'
needs, are common in urban areas.

❖ **Competition and Adaptation**

In a sense, humans and native wildlife are competing for their preferred habitat—lush, grassy
yards for humans versus native habitat for
wildlife. Obviously, humans could easily win
this battle. However, if humans consider the
needs of specialists when developing urban
areas, native wildlife can also win.

Humans may be the only species that can
afford to show concern for another species.
For most animals *competition* is a struggle for
survival. They compete for resources, such as
food, water, shelter, and space, in amounts that
will allow them to survive. Species with similar
requirements for food, nest sites, den sites,
and/or other needs are the most likely to

House Sparrow

compete. However, it is only when resources are limited that intense competitive battles erupt.

When competition among species is intense and remains that way for a long time, a number of things can happen. One species can drive a competing species away. For example, ecologists believe that aggressive starlings drive northern flickers away when they live in the same habitat. This is an example of *interference competition*. Starlings directly interfere with flickers' attempts to secure habitat by driving them away from nest holes. Another type of competition is *exploitative competition*, in which species indirectly compete for resources. When house sparrows and house finches occupy the same area, they compete in this manner. House finches *exploit*, or use efficiently or intensively, the resources needed by both, leaving less for house sparrows. The result is the number of house sparrows declines due to inadequate nutrition and less reproduction.

Species may also adapt in ways that allow them to divide up the resources instead of competing for them. The famous scientist Charles Darwin studied twelve species of finches in the Galapagos Islands. Each had a slightly different beak shape and size. He attributed these differences to adaptations for exploiting the variety of foods that occur on the islands. Adaptations like these, which allow animals to partition resources, may explain why some species with similar needs have slightly different physical or behavioral traits.

However, just because certain animals have different physical or behavioral traits and appear to

American Robin

share one or more resources, does not mean that these traits arose because of competition. For example, one can not assume that the birds in the backyard picture were ever in competition with one another, despite the fact that they all eat insects. Robins, yellow warblers, and brown creepers probably adapted to their environment independently of each other. The fact that each species locates its insect prey in a different place (and is adapted to finding it there) is likely to be a mere coincidence. Nevertheless, these adaptations are fascinating.

Robins find most of their prey just beneath the soil's surface. Their long, sturdy beaks are helpful for pulling earthworms and insects out of the ground. Yellow warblers glean insects from leaves and twigs of small trees and shrubs. They are light and quick, which allows them to feed at the end of slender branches. Brown creepers find insects and their larvae on or under the bark of old trees. They have sharp claws for clinging to tree trunks and thin, pointed beaks for poking into bark crevices.

Each of these species obtains different kinds of insects from different sites (ground, leaves, and bark). Although these adaptations may not be a result of past competition, they may help the species avoid direct competition for food now. Where an animal finds its prey is part of its ecological niche. Having different niches may help decrease competition among species.

❖ **Food Chains and the Web of Life**

When describing what animals eat, and what eats them, you are describing *food chains*. A broader and more realistic concept is called the *web of life*. In the web, as in nature, food chains overlap. In addition, the web of life is made up of non-living elements such as water, air, sun, soil, rocks, and chemicals, which interact with the wildlife community. It may help to picture a food chain or the web of life by organizing the species in the backyard illustration into groups of producers and consumers. *Producers*, as the name suggests, produce or make food. On the other hand, *consumers* consume or use what the producers make, usually by eating it. Food chains and the web of life are made up of producers and consumers.

Plants are producers. Their main source of energy is the sun. They capture the sun's energy and turn it into food that animals can eat. Leaves are the sites of food production.

Animals, of course, can not make their own food; they must eat plants and/or animals to survive. The animals that eat plants, or plant parts such as seeds and roots, are the first level of consumers. They are called *herbivores*. In our summer scene, cottontails are the main herbivores. The second level of consumers eat animals. They are called *carnivores*. Insect-eaters are called *insectivores*, but they are often described as carnivores because insects are animals, too. The domestic cat, although not a wild animal, is an active carnivore in the urban ecosystem. The garter snake, yellow warbler, and brown creeper are primarily insectivores. *Omnivores* are animals that during any one season or the course of a year eat both plants and animals,

including insects. The omnivores in the picture are the blue jay, robin, tiger swallowtail, and raccoon.

A simple food chain in this backyard, for example, starts with the grass, which uses the sun's energy to grow. The second link in the chain is the cottontail, which eats the grass. The domestic cat might provide the third and final link by preying upon a young cottontail. In the wild, a hawk or coyote would be a more likely predator of cottontails than the domestic cat.

Garter Snake

It is more realistic to view an ecosystem as a web of life, rather than as a series of unrelated food chains. For instance, other species besides the cottontail depend on grass. The garter snake uses it for protective cover and a place to prey on insects. In addition, dense grass keeps the moisture in the soil. As a result, the robin is easily able to find insects and worms just beneath the soil's surface.

You may want to identify the food chains and web of life that exist in your backyard, schoolyard, or alleyway. If so, think about how the chains overlap each other and what roles sunlight, water, air, soil, and rocks play in the animals' lives. Most importantly, think about the roles that you play now and that other persons have played in the past. How do you think the web of life has changed since your city was built, since your neighborhood was developed, or since you were born? How can humans insure that the web stays intact and the ecosystem continues to function?

❖ Conclusion

Urbanization results in habitat alteration which, in turn, affects wildlife. Humans, of course, are responsible for habitat alteration. To a certain extent it is justified. Society dictates that people have places to live, work, and play, and have roads on which to travel. Creating these things inevitably alters the habitat of other animals. However, people should strive to minimize the amount of habitat they alter. Considering the habitat and resource needs of other species and applying the concept of limiting factors are necessary steps to help preserve wildlife habitat in and near cites.

SUMMER
BACKYARD
HABITAT

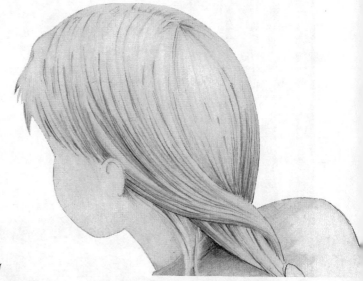

Human Being

CHAPTER 8

BACKYARD HABITAT IN THE WINTER

*I*t's a circus outside on a winter day, or so it seems. This backyard scene is very different from the previous one. The quiet days of summer have been replaced by a frenzy of winter feeding. If you compare the winter and summer backyard pictures you will notice that many of the species are different. Seasonal changes in community composition are typical in Colorado and throughout the world.

WINTER
BACKYARD
HABITAT

*Black-
Capped
Chickadee*

Behavioral Adaptations

Changes in community composition are due in part to *migration*, the movement of animals from one place to another. Migration is a *behavioral adaptation* for coping with the snow and cold of winter. Behavioral adaptations are ways that animals act that help them survive in their environment. Animals migrate for feeding and breeding purposes. Birds are the most common migrators, but many other types of animals migrate, too. For example, tarantulas (spiders), salmon (fish), box turtles (reptiles), pronghorns (mammals), and monarch butterflies (insects) migrate every year. Some species travel short distances, while others travel many miles.

The bison, a native mammal of Colorado, was also once a migrator. Vast herds of bison moved across the plains, grazing the grass in one area and moving on to the next, allowing the grazed areas to recover. There are few wild bison now. However, even if there were more, barriers such as fences, subdivisions, interstate highways, and croplands would prevent their movement. For many species, migration paths and their destinations are becoming increasingly obstructed. Highways and roads are treacherous for small animals traveling on foot. Migrating birds and butterflies are not having an easy time either. Although air travel might be easier than ground travel, these migrators are having difficulty finding suit-

Bison

able habitat during and at the end of their journey. For example, many songbirds migrate to the tropics each winter in search of insects. However, more and more of their winter habitats—tropical rainforests and brushlands are being destroyed. Nations must work together to preserve both summer and winter habitats of migrating birds. If not, songbirds, like the yellow warbler, may not return to our backyards in the springtime.

WINTER BACKYARD HABITAT

House Finch

Other birds in Colorado migrate between the highlands in summer and the lowlands in winter. For example, black-capped chickadees, white-breasted nuthatches, downy woodpeckers, and dark-eyed juncos live in the mountain forests during summer. In the fall these birds move down to the foothills and into the urban areas on the plains for winter. During the cold winter months they are common in suburbs where they eat sunflower seeds (chickadees) and suet (nuthatches and downy woodpeckers).

In some parts of the country blue jays migrate in flocks of fifty to one hundred. In Colorado, though, they rarely migrate. Therefore, the blue jay scolding the fox squirrel in the winter backyard scene could very well be the same bird eating seeds in the summer scene. House finches are also year-round residents in Colorado. Like blue jays, they are non-natives that depend on urban environments for their needs.

Perhaps the most confusing of Colorado's migratory birds is the robin. It is hard to know whether they are coming or going. Actually, they are doing both! Many of the robins that spend summer in Colorado migrate south for winter. When they leave,

*Evening
Grosbeak*

robins from up north fly south to Colorado. In other words, there are robins along the Front Range throughout the year; however, only a few are year-round residents. The saying that a robin is the first sign of spring simply does not apply in Colorado.

By now you probably recognize that there are many different types of migration. Evening grosbeaks have a unique migration style, too. Like chickadees, nuthatches, and downy woodpeckers, they migrate up and down mountain slopes. However, they sometimes migrate south for the winter when the fall production of plant seeds has been low. Poor seed crops may happen as often as every other year.

*Bohemian
Waxwing*

On occasion bohemian waxwings migrate to Colorado for the winter months. A juniper tree laden with berries or a platform feeder covered with raisins may attract them to your yard. These birds look more like a band of masqueraders than a flock of hungry birds, and at close range they are a beautiful sight. They have a crest of soft brown feathers, a tiny black mask on their faces, and delicate red and yellow coloration on their wings.

Migration is one of many behavioral adaptations for winter. Others adaptations include when cottontails seek shelter from the wind in clumps of evergreen shrubs, when chickadees huddle in a tree *cavity,* or hole, to keep warm, or when birds flock together to increase their chances of finding food. Another way in which some species survive food shortages in winter is to cache seeds and dead insects before they become scarce. Later, as winter progresses and food is harder to find, these birds remember where their hidden meals are. Chickadees, jays, and nuthatches are all food-cachers.

❖ Physiological Adaptations

In addition to behavioral adaptations, animals have *physiological adaptations* for coping with the cold weather and decreased food supply of winter. Physiological adaptations are ways that an animal's body prepares for certain environmental conditions. For example, some mammals grow an extra coat of dense fur for the winter. Other animals, usually small ones, enter *torpor*. Torpor is a short-term condition in which body temperatures drop and heart and breathing rates slow down. When an animal is in torpor it requires less food. Chipmunks spend most of the winter in torpor, usually holed up in a snug burrow. However, on warm winter days they often come above ground to feed or sun themselves. Black-capped chickadees also enter torpor, but only when the temperature drops to freezing or below.

Hibernation is another way in which some animals survive cold winters. It is similar to torpor in that body temperatures drop, and heart and breathing rates slow down; however, hibernation is a long-term condition. Hibernators don't come out until spring arrives. In Colorado, the true hibernators are reptiles, amphibians, and some mammals, such as bats and many species of ground squirrels. Insects have a strategy similar to hibernation, called *diapause*. Scientists believe that both hiber-

Nuthatch

nation and diapause begin and end when there is a significant change in weather and day length.

The flurry of activity around the winter bird feeders may be misleading. If you compare the number of animals in the winter and summer backyard scenes, you might conclude that animal populations are largest during winter. This is usually not the case. Animal numbers are typically highest during midsummer. This is the time when most of the young have been born, or have hatched, and before many of them have been eaten by predators. The high number of animals in the winter scene may simply be a result of many animals congregating around a limited winter resource—food. Of course, animals may also seem more abundant in the winter because they are easier to see when the trees and shrubs are bare.

The number of animals differs not only among seasons, but also among inner cities, suburbs, and rural areas. Some scientists think that the sheer number of animals in suburbs and cities is higher than in the surrounding countryside. They attribute this abundance to the presence of generalist species, such as starlings and raccoons. Generalists readily adjust to new habitats. They take advantage of urban conditions, like the surplus of waste-food, the availability of shelter, fertilized grass and shrubs, and for many species, the scarcity of predators. As a result, populations of generalist species flourish in cities. Industrialized inner cities may provide an exception—they have few animals because all types of food, even waste-food, are scarce.

❖ Wildlife Diversity

In addition to the numbers of animals, many scientists think that the *diversity,* or variety, of animals is greater in the urban ecosystem than elsewhere. In other words, they think that urban areas, including suburbs, contain more species than most rural and wilderness areas. They cite the availability of both native and new habitats as the primary reason. These habitats are colonized by the native species that can adjust to urban conditions and by the generalists that call urban areas home.

Black-Capped Chickadee

For example, in this backyard there is a great diversity of native and non-native birds and mammals. Black-capped chickadees, evening grosbeaks, white-breasted nuthatches, downy woodpeckers, bohemian waxwings, cottontail rabbits (note the tracks), and juncos are all natives of Colorado. The overall diversity of species, though, is increased by the non-native generalists—blue jays, fox squirrels, and house finches.

Among other animals, such as insects, spiders, reptiles, and amphibians, a high diversity may be less likely in urban areas than elsewhere. The habitats of these animals are often smaller and more restricted to a specific habitat than those of mammals and birds. As a result, they are especially vulnerable to destruction during urban development.

❖ Native Versus Non-native Species Diversity

The loss of any native species, whether a mammal or an insect, causes a loss of native species diversity. The term that many ecologists use to describe the diversity of native species and ecosystems is biological diversity

Fox Squirrel

or *biodiversity*. Even if attracting or introducing non-natives brings about higher overall diversity, many people would argue that preserving biodiversity is more important.

For example, ecologists might say that non-native species have the potential to displace populations of native species. Or that some non-natives are carriers of diseases and parasites to which many natives are susceptible. In addition, they might argue that native species, unlike non-natives, have evolved with their habitats for thousands or millions of years. As a result, their *genes,* or hereditary material passed from parent to offspring, are better equipped to respond to changes in the natural environment. Along this same line, they might discuss the importance of preserving all of a species' genetic diversity. A particular gene in a particular population just may hold the cure to cancer, or it may have a special application to science, industry, or agriculture. Another reason they might offer is that native animals and plants give an area its identity. A unique identity provides aesthetic, educational, and economic benefits.

Of course, other people could counter these points with thoughts of their own. Some might say that lush lawns and shade trees are worth the loss of some native habitat and perhaps even species. Or they might make the point that urban environments create ecological niches which, if filled by non-natives, may not threaten native species. For example, fox squirrels have made their niche in the hardwood trees planted in Front Range cities. Still others might say that they are glad that non-native habitats were created because they have attracted some beautiful animals like the blue jay. In addition, they might argue that house sparrows and fox squirrels have as much right to be here as most humans do, because other than Native Americans, Coloradans are non-natives, too.

As always, there are at least two sides to every debate. You may be opposed to establishing non-native habitats and attracting and introducing non-native species, or you may support these actions. Or your sentiments may fall somewhere in between. What is certain is that your opinion about this and other environmental issues will influence the future of wildlife in Colorado. Even if you are too young to vote, your opinions undoubtedly affect your actions and influence the attitudes of people around you. For these reasons it is important that you consider the facts about wildlife conservation and develop your own set of values.

❖ Bird Feeding

The owners of the house in this picture are participating in one of America's booming hobbies—bird feeding. In the United States, approximately one out of every six households feeds birds regularly. Those who sprinkle the seed, hang the suet, fill the feeders, and offer the fruit do so because they love birds. Bird feeding provides bird lovers an opportunity to observe the beauty and behavior of their subjects up close.

Downy Woodpecker

What's in it for the birds? This is a question that many urban ecologists are asking. They are coming up with some answers, but there is much more to learn about the effects of artificial feeding on birds. In general, though, ecologists believe that the

74

advantages of bird feeding far outweigh the disadvantages.

One myth about bird feeding is that
birds will become dependent on human
handouts. The concern is that they will
die of starvation if the feeding were to
stop. This is a myth because the diets of
birds are rarely dominated by feeder food.
In general, even the regulars at your bird
feeder balance their diets with plant seeds and
insects throughout the year.

During winter, bird feeding has the greatest potential to influence bird populations.
Even then, only minor population declines of
certain species would occur if, for example, all
bird feeders suddenly became empty. One
study concludes that bird feeding reduces the
number of starvation-related deaths only
when temperatures drop below −15 degrees
Farenheit for an extended period of time.
Along the Front Range, temperatures this
cold are rare. Nevertheless, it is likely that
bird feeding gives birds a boost when the
snow begins to fall and blankets their natural
food sources. Also, birds that have supple-
mented their normal winter diets with feeder
food may be in better shape for the spring
breeding season.

Lucky are the birds that land in this backyard. There is something for everyone! These
homeowners offer their visitors a variety of
foods, such as black oil sunflower seed, *suet,*
or soft chunks of animal fat, native berries,
millet seed, apple slices, and raisins. They also
separate the foods into different feeders,
which helps to reduce competition among the
birds. In addition, they provide food on the
ground as well as on raised platforms and in

hanging feeders. They do this because different species prefer different heights for feeding. The trees and shrubs provide perch sites and escape shelter from the occasional hawk or cat. However, they also provide ambush sites for these same predators. Placing feeders and birdbaths at least four feet from vegetation is a good way to prevent predation on backyard wildlife.

❖ Seasonal Changes in Bird Requirements

Feeding probably has its greatest influence on bird populations during the winter. However, each season brings a new set of energy demands. If you decide to feed birds throughout the year you will have more success if you are sensitive to their changing needs. Whether you feed birds or not, knowing their seasonal demands and requirements lends insight into their relationships with plants, other animals, and the physical environment.

For example, early spring is a tough time for birds in Colorado. Most of the natural foods like nuts, seeds, and berries have been eaten and the insects have not yet emerged. A late snow could cause some birds to starve to death. Furthermore, birds that are migrating through the state on their way to their breeding grounds need ample food and water for their long flights. If you provide food and water, as well as adequate shelter and space, you probably will attract spring migrants as they pass through Colorado. You may also attract breeding birds looking for a place to build their nests.

Bohemian Waxwing

During summer, foods such as insects and early-ripening fruits are abundant, as are the food requirements of both young and adult birds. The rapid growth rate of nestlings requires a high protein diet best offered by a steady supply of insects. Even seed-eating adults feed their young a diet mostly of insects. A source of high protein that you can provide is a mixture of two parts cornmeal, and one part each of peanut butter, flour, and vegetable shortening. In summer, this mixture is a better source of protein than suet because it will not turn rancid in the heat. Fruit-loving birds such as colorful tanagers, orioles, and certain woodpeckers can be enticed into your backyard by offering over-ripe bananas and opened oranges on a platform feeder.

In late summer and early fall naturally-occurring foods continue to be abundant. Insects are still active and the fruits of many plants are ripe. A plentiful food source is just what *fledglings*, birds just learning to fly, need because growing and flying require lots of energy. Also during this time most birds *molt*, or drop their old feathers and grow new ones, another energy demanding process. As fall progresses, many songbirds, shorebirds, and waterfowl prepare for migration. Before leaving, they eat a lot of food and put on weight. By providing a ready source of food, you may help birds meet the energy demands of a long migration.

Excellent information is available about how to attract birds to your property and which foods to provide. You may want to check the suggested readings list in the back of the book for references.

❖ Conclusion

Just like humans, animals have special needs that vary throughout the year and throughout a lifetime. Charting an animal's energy demands and habitat needs over the course of a year or a lifetime is an interesting activity. It is likely that you will find out the basics— what that animal needs, why it needs these particular things, and where it finds them. More important is the appreciation you will develop for the way an animal interacts with its environment.

CHAPTER 9

RIPARIAN HABITAT IN THE SPRING

Winter is over. The only snow left is high in the mountains where the sun is gradually turning it to water. In thousands of little streams melted flakes join together for a mad rush down the mountainsides. Throughout late spring and summer these streams are busy rushing water to the foothills. There they spill into and swell Front Range rivers such as the South Platte, the Arkansas, the Cache La Poudre, and the Saint Vrain. Year after year these slow-moving rivers carry the water out of the mountains and across the thirsty plains.

As rivers move overland, their banks soak up water and store it in the soil, in aquatic plants, and in the roots of trees. The earth and plants begin to pulse with life and the animals respond. Insects emerge, many of them timed with the growth of particular plants or the blossoming of certain flowers. Bats arise from their winter roosts to feed on flying insects in the evening air. A fish strikes the water's surface for insect larvae, only to be struck itself by the sharp beak of a hungry heron. A deer *browses,* or eats the tips of, willows and other shrubs that grow beside the river. And humans come out to enjoy the return of migrating birds.

In Colorado's cities there is perhaps no better place to witness the rebirth of spring and the interactions of nature than near the river's edge. Rivers and the lands that border them are called *riparian corridors. Habitat corridors*, of which riparian corridors are a subset, are strips of land that differ from the habitats surrounding them. Other examples of habitat corridors are strips of shortgrass prairie along fence rows, swaths of evergreen trees between shopping malls, and mowed areas beneath power lines. Habitat corridors are extremely beneficial to animal populations.

❖ **Riparian Corridors and Home Ranges**

As you can tell by looking at the preceding habitat picture, riparian corridors are popular places for wildlife. They provide abundant habitat. Some animals, such as coyotes, mule deer, and black-billed magpies, spend part of their lives in riparian zones, but they are not restricted to them. Others, like beaver and fish, depend on riparian corridors for all of their habitat needs. The smallest area in which an animal finds adequate food, water, shelter, and space is called a *home range.* Home ranges vary in size depending on the animal, its sex, the season of the year, and the quality of habitat. In general, smaller home ranges indicate higher quality habitat for individuals of a particular species.

The home range of the beaver in the picture may stretch for a mile or more along this river. Beavers live in small family groups. Within their home range, a mother beaver, her newborn kits, and her *yearlings,* or last year's young, find all of their requirements for living. The father beaver spends much of his time in the mother's home range, but his home range is even larger and extends farther upstream. Watching members of a beaver family meet their survival needs is a lesson in physical and behavioral adaptations.

On first sight, what looks like a large, awkward mammal is really a master lumberjack, top-notch swimmer, and a brilliant engineer. With their powerful feet, beavers dig dens in the riverbank. Many beavers will build stick and mud lodges instead of dens. Their dens and lodges have underwater entrances. In late spring, dens and lodges serve as nurseries where beavers rear their kits. During winter, when ice covers the river, they are transformed into dining rooms. The pantries are stashes of sticks with each stick rammed into the mud at the bottom of the river. When beavers are hungry, they swim out, pull up a stick or two, return to the den, and position themselves beside

Beaver and Kits

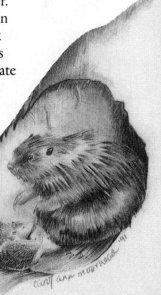

the entrance. As they nibble, the scraps fall into the water and the current carries them away. Once spring comes, beavers prefer to eat leaves and the tender new growth of trees. With their agile forefeet, beavers fold individual leaves into their mouths and roll the thin sticks back and forth to expose their tastier parts.

For beavers in the riparian corridors of the plains, much of the spring diet comes from the tops of tall cottonwood trees. Instead of climbing up to reach the branches, beavers bring the tasty new growth down to the ground by felling the entire tree! This task is made possible by adaptations such as large front teeth, which continue to grow as they are worn down, and strong jaw muscles and bones that can withstand the constant gnawing of wood.

After the leaves and new growth are eaten, beavers rarely leave trees to rot. Instead, they push and pull the branches, and occasionally the trunks, into the river where they use them to build dams. The dams back up the water and create deeper pools. Deep water allows beavers to travel to and from their food supplies safely. Their large hind feet, webbed toes, and flat, flipper-like tails make swimming easy for these underwater engineers.

As you probably already know, other species with home ranges in riparian corridors are fish. Black bullheads (a type of catfish), white suckers, green sunfish, and fathead minnows are common in Front Range rivers and streams. They are all generalists— able to adapt to a variety of conditions including polluted

Black
Bullhead

and murky water. These species form an
urban fish community. In other words, in
streams where you find one of these fish you
will often find the others. However, they do
occupy different places within the stream.

Black bullheads avoid ripples and fast-mov-
ing currents. They live in the still waters of
eddies and pools. An ideal nesting spot for
bullheads is a muddy river bottom beneath a
fallen log. Fathead minnows and green sunfish also prefer quiet or slow-flowing water.
White suckers have a different strategy. They
spawn, or lay their eggs, on gravel in moving
water. As you can imagine, their eggs rarely
stay put. Instead, they drift downstream until
they get caught on a rock, log, or stem of an
aquatic plant. If you want to find
white suckers, look near boul-
ders, bridge abutments, and under-
cut banks where the water is flowing fairly
fast. Note that in the picture the white suckers are swimming up the middle of the river—
where the current is generally fastest.

*White
Suckers*

❖ Ecological Interactions

River ecology is fun to study. Even on a short
stretch of river like the one illustrated, thousands of community and ecosystem interactions are taking place. Some of these interactions you can see in a single afternoon of sit-
ting on the riverbank. Others are so subtle,
obscured, or microscopic that you can only
imagine that they are happening. For example, in the time it takes to read this sentence,
a fathead minnow might be sucking down a
black bullhead's egg. Typically one
black bullhead parent swims guard
over the nest, but despite this

Green Sunfish

precaution, minnows and sunfish manage to steal their share of eggs. Another species, the green sunfish, has a large mouth, which enables it to eat many sizes of prey. These fish are as likely to eat minnows as they are bullhead eggs.

You may be wondering what black bullheads and white suckers eat. Fish biologists call them bottom feeders because they feed at the bottom of streams and ponds. Their tastes are far from finicky; they simply filter the silt and gravel in search of immature insects and plant material.

Another bottom feeder is the mallard, a common duck. Have you ever wondered what mallards are doing when they tip bottom up? They, too, are feeding on the bottom.

Mallard

However, mallards look mainly for seeds. They feed on seeds from a wide array of plants including bulrush, pondweed, smartweed, and some trees. Although mallards prefer seeds, they also eat fish eggs, small fish, tadpoles, aquatic insects, snails, and tender plant parts.

❖ Pollutants in the Food Chain

Being a bottom feeder can have its drawbacks. In urban or agricultural areas, pollutants are widespread. Gas, oil, antifreeze, household cleaners, pesticides, and herbicides are some of the more common pollutants. Others are excess nitrogen and phosphorus from fertilizers, and sulfur dioxide and other contaminants spewed into the air by cars and smoke stacks. All of these eventually make their way to rivers. Once in the river, they do

not simply go away. Instead, they make their
way into the sediments at the bottom of the
river. In a classic example of an ecosystem
interaction, the pollutants enter food chains
via the sediments. If the pollutants become
concentrated or toxic enough the results can
be tragic.

*Fathead
Minnows*

   Consider a tale of a pollutant passing
through the riparian community pictured earlier. A great blue heron has found a new
stretch of river, unfortunately polluted, where
the hunting has been great. Over a period of
weeks he has speared and gulped down many
fish. His favorites are fathead minnows, but
he has also eaten a number of tainted young
black bullheads and white suckers, which had
been feeding in the contaminated sediments
at the bottom of the river. The pollutants,
which were initially in the sediments and were
passed up the food chain, are now fully incor-
porated into the body of the heron. One day
while the heron stands still, concentrating on
the water for an unsuspecting fish to pass by,
a hungry coyote steals up from behind and
leaps from the bank. As the coyote makes a
meal of the heron, the chemicals are
passed farther up the food chain.
Late that winter the coyote dies,
perhaps from old age, harsh weather,
chemical contamination, or a combination of these factors. On a sandbar by the
river, its body is easily spotted by a passing
magpie. Before you know it, five or six
magpies are hopping around the carcass and
picking at the flesh, passing the chemicals
along yet another time. The chemicals
left in the carcass will gradually leach
into the sandbar and be washed back

Great Blue Heron

into the sediments at the bottom of the river. There they will start the cycle all over again.

The chemical culprits of death and decreasing populations are often hard to identify. Around the world, scientists and naturalists are reporting the decline and disappearance of many species of amphibians. In Colorado, the once abundant northern leopard frog is becoming rare. Its increasing rarity may be due to predation by the ever-growing numbers of bullfrogs, a non-native species. However, northern leopard frogs are becoming scarce even in areas where bullfrogs do not exist. Could acid rain be the culprit? Because of the *global*, or worldly, nature of the amphibian declines, some scientists think so. No one can be sure until more research is done.

Can you imagine a world without frogs? Beginning in April of each year, northern leopard frogs and striped chorus frogs fill the air above rivers, marshes, and ponds with croaks, snores, and trills. Without them, warm spring evenings would be hauntingly quiet. In addition to their calls, people would miss the frogs' endless appetites for insects. Without frogs there would be many more of the problems associated with insect outbreaks, such as disease, illness, and annoyance.

❖ **Wildlife Preservation**

Far easier to imagine than a world without frogs is a world in which people take action to protect frogs, and other species, too.

Although the cause of amphibian declines is not known, you can bet that

pollution and habitat loss are not helping. One of the best ways to decrease the amount of pollution in the environment is to stop creating it. There are many ways you can do this, including recycling, using environmentally safe products, and asking your elected officials to support clean air and clean water legislation.

89

RIPARIAN
HABITAT
IN SPRING

*Northern
Leopard
Frog*

Although some species of reptiles and amphibians do well in cities, the majority of native ones decline as a result of urbanization. Preserving habitat is usually the most effective way to save species, perhaps even for the northern leopard frog. However, habitat preservation is no small feat, especially in and around cities. To fully appreciate the need for habitat preservation, it may help to have a better understanding of habitat destruction. Rarely does the term habitat destruction signify the complete loss of a particular kind of habitat. Usually it refers to the partial destruction of a habitat type. Exceptions may be rare habitats, those small pockets of land where the environmental conditions are unique, to which certain (often rare) species of amphibians, reptiles, invertebrates, and plants have adapted.

❖ Habitat Fragmentation

Ecologists refer to the partial destruction of habitats as *habitat fragmentation*, a process by which large habitat types are broken into pieces. To help you understand this process, picture yourself punching holes in a piece of paper with a hole punch. Think of the untouched paper as a natural, undeveloped habitat. As you begin to punch, imagine that the little dots of falling paper are parcels of destroyed habitat. In each of the holes picture housing developments, hospitals, shopping malls, roads, parking lots, and agricultural fields. As you punch more and more holes notice how the paper becomes weaker and loses some or most of its function. Finally, when the paper is riddled with holes, focus on what remains between the holes. Envision these areas as patches of habitat and corridors linking them. In the real world isolated habitat patches without corridors are common — these are called *habitat islands.*

This process of hole-punching or habitat fragmentation has taken place in habitats around the world. Scientists are beginning to learn what effects this process is having on the species that live in these habitats. You may have heard about *tropical deforestation.* In the tropics, holes are being punched in rain forests at an alarming rate as forests are cut and/or burned down. There are more species of plants and animals in the tropics than anywhere else in the world, and many of these species have small or rare habitats. Consequently, losing habitat from even a small parcel of land may result in the extinction of hundreds of species.

The hardwood forests of the eastern United States are also being fragmented. Biologists are noticing population declines in a number of forest-interior birds, those songbirds that require nesting sites deep within forests. Many of these same birds spend their winters in the fragmented tropics. To ensure the survival of songbirds and other species, nations all over the world must work together to preserve summer and winter habitat for migratory birds.

Prairie Dog

In Colorado the shortgrass prairie has had a similar history to that of the hole-punched paper. Before the farming era, the prairie stretched for miles and miles, interrupted only by an occasional river. Activities during the farming and urban eras have fragmented the shortgrass prairie and left only remnants of original habitat. Undoubtedly, many species of insects, spiders, and plants have been lost as the prairie has been turned under for crops and urban development. Other species, such as badgers, prairie dogs, and prairie chickens (a kind of grouse) have suffered population declines. However, not many bird or mammal species have gone extinct. Their survival is due to many factors: the ability of these species to adjust to agricultural and urban environments, the preservation of some grassland habitat, and the maintenance of habitat corridors.

❖ The Importance of Habitat Corridors

Preserving and creating habitat corridors are perhaps the most effective ways to maintain wildlife populations in fragmented habitats. Before singing the praises of corridors, though, you should know that corridors are not always beneficial to wildlife. Creating a corridor into a previously isolated habitat could be disastrous for certain species. A newly created corridor might provide passage for predators or disease to which the animal populations in the isolated area are not adapted, causing them to go extinct.

However, in most cases corridors play an important role because they serve as wildlife "highways" among patches of fragmented habitat. Permitting movement between habi-

tat frag-
ments is
perhaps
the great-
est benefit
of corridors.
Immigration is
the movement of an ani-
mal from one habitat area
to another. In the late summer or
fall, many young animals leave their parents'
home ranges to find their own, a process
known as *dispersal*. In fragmented environments, habitat corridors make immigration
and dispersal possible for many species. These
movements, as well as seasonal and daily
movements between habitat areas, keep animal populations healthy.

Immigration and dispersal prevent over-
crowding of habitat, help potential mates find
each other, and promote *gene flow*. Gene flow
is the movement of genes through a population as a result of reproduction. When it is
restricted, animal populations gradually
become inbred and unable to adapt to new
environmental conditions. When it is unre-
stricted, the *gene pool*
remains diverse. The
term gene pool
refers collectively to
all the genes of a popu-
lation. A diverse gene
pool, in turn, enables a population to adapt over time to
changes in the environ-
ment.

Large blocks of habitat
on the outskirts of town are

Mule Deer

known as *source areas*. Source areas are usually in good condition and large enough to sustain an adequate gene flow for the wildlife populations that live there. Small habitat fragments, often inside city limits, are called *recipient areas*. They may be too small to permit adequate gene flow, especially over time. Populations in recipient areas may survive, though, if animals from source areas move in and add diversity to the gene pool. Movement from source areas to recipient areas, especially for animals on foot, would not be possible without habitat corridors.

The riparian corridor in the picture connects the foothills on the west side of town with the plains on the eastern edge of town. Within city limits it links together parks and open spaces. Small animals travel only short distances in the corridor, while others, such as the mule deer, travel miles. The mule deer in this picture is on her way back to the foothills where she will spend the summer. During the winter she found food and protection from cold weather in the lowland riparian habitat. Mule deer are an uncommon sight on the eastern side of Front Range cities simply because the riparian corridors are not adequately protected as they pass through urban areas.

Coyotes also travel long distances along habitat corridors. These generalists are one of the most successful colonizers of urban habitats. Corridors connect sites at which coyotes find their various habitat needs. In this picture the coyote has found a place to drink and a grassy field where he catches his mainstays— mice, cottontails, and voles (often called meadow mice). Up the river he dens in a hollow log on the edge

Vole

Coyote

of a city park. Sometimes he ventures into suburbs or even the heart of the city looking for food in garbage cans.

Habitat corridors also benefit humans. Many corridors are peaceful places, removed from the frantic pace and noise of the city. They offer people who visit them solitude and a chance to reflect on their lives and rekindle their spirits. In addition, corridors provide excellent places to watch birds and wildlife.

❖ Benefits of Wildlife Watching

In the spring, wildlife watching has some special rewards. Not only will you see young of the year, you may also find where they were born or where they hatched from their eggs. Finding bird nests is particularly fun because each one is an architectural wonder. In the picture there are five different species of birds, each of which builds a different style of nest. For example, hanging from a branch in the foreground is the northern oriole's nest. Orioles are extraordinary weavers. To make its nest, the northern oriole weaves plant fibers and shreds of bark into a pouch about six inches deep. The female lines the inside with horsehair and soft materials such as sheep's wool, fine mosses, and plant down. Look for these woven cradles in trees along riparian corridors or beside lakes, anywhere from six to fifty feet above the ground. Between April and June it's likely that three to six eggs are rocking safely inside.

*Belted
Kingfishe*

The belted kingfisher's nest is much harder to find than the oriole's. It is located in the riverbank at the end of a tunnel. Digging with their beaks and feet, the male and female kingfisher spend almost three weeks in the spring excavating a nest tunnel and chamber for their young. The chamber is usually littered with little white bones and scales from fish, their favorite food.

Magpie

Another bird that hides its nest well is the mallard duck. It builds a large, cup-like nest of leaves and downy feathers in a variety of places. The nest may be close to shore, nestled in dead grasses, or at the base of a hollow tree.

Great blue herons and black-billed magpies have large, conspicuous nests. Although both make their nests primarily out of sticks, the nests are shaped very differently. In the background of the picture you can see a heron *rookery,* a place where individuals of the same species nest together. If you look carefully, you can see that the nests are large, flat platforms. Each year great blue herons repair and reuse these flimsy nests, and each year they get bigger. Some are as wide as four feet. Herons line their nests with twigs, marsh grasses, and cattail leaves.

Magpie nests are built to last. At first glance, these sturdy structures look like a large ball of sticks. On closer inspection, though, you will notice that they have a roof, side entrance, and a bottom fortified with mud. The nest cups are lined with horsehair, fine roots, and soft plant stems. Other birds will sometimes "rent out" the roofs of magpie nests and build their own nests right on top. Wood ducks and even cats have been known to occupy abandoned magpie nests.

Big Brown Bat

Another reward for wildlife watchers in spring is the erratic flights of bats. Although many species of bats in

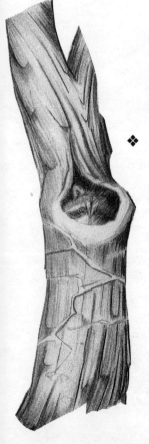

Colorado are migratory and return from Central and South America in the spring, some of the common urban bats simply emerge from local hibernation roosts. The bats you are likely to see flying in your neighborhood or above the local river are year-round residents of Colorado and are called big brown bats. They leave their daytime roosts (hollow trees and attics) at dusk to begin their nightly feeding routines.

Similar to radar detectors that detect the speed of cars, bats have built-in sonar detectors that sense the direction and range of flying insects. Bats emit high-pitched sounds that travel through the air, bounce off the nearest object, and bounce back to their big ears. In less than a second they can detect and catch an insect. Scientists believe that bats eat thousands of insects each hour. It is no wonder that many people are putting up bat houses in their yards. One bat is far more effective, economical, and beneficial to the environment than a can of insecticide.

❖ **Conclusion**

Riparian corridors are one of the most significant habitats in urban areas because they provide the links between habitat patches. Along the Front Range, the rivers that run through these corridors are the common threads that weave together mountain, foothills, and prairie habitats. Protecting riparian corridors preserves the natural migration routes of many species and the aquatic habitat of rivers. In addition, their protection preserves the area's most fertile land, Colorado's most valuable wildlife habitat, as well as treasured getaways for urban dwellers.

Raccoon

CHAPTER 10
PARK AND OPEN SPACE HABITAT IN FALL

It's almost noon these days before the sun takes the chill out of the air. Leaves are brown and curling inward at the edges. Some of the cottonwoods and poplars are turning a deep, burning yellow. Whenever the slightest breeze blows, their delicate leaves catch and throw the sunlight in every direction. Yesterday a flock of geese floated up off the ground and settled down again. All day they were stretching their wings and craning their necks, limbering up for the day when they lift off and head south for the winter. Fall has arrived.

A few years ago the park in this picture looked very different. Other than the distant cottonwoods, there was little native vegetation. Turf grass encircled the entire pond. The few trees that were planted were spindly and spaced far apart. Fox squirrels, flickers, and skunks rarely visited the park and when they did they usually moved on to find better habitat. Other than geese and ducks, there were only a few species, including humans, that used this park.

❖ Planning a Park

It was also a few years ago that the city parks supervisor began receiving requests from local residents for more wildlife watching opportunities in the park. Before taking any action the supervisor decided to consult a wildlife biologist. After studying the park, the biologist suggested some short- and long-range plans to improve wildlife watching. Both she and the park supervisor agreed that park planning could best be done by a team of experts. In other words, two heads (or more) are better than one. Within a month they had formed a committee that consisted of an aquatic ecologist, a landscape architect, an urban planner, and themselves. They were pleased with the committee because each member was committed to bringing urbanites into closer contact with nature.

At their first meeting the committee members shared their ideas and concerns about the park. The landscape architect suggested keeping over half of the park in its well-groomed condition, but encouraging the remaining area to go wild. He recommended planting native trees and shrubs throughout the park, including the groomed areas. He also mentioned the possibility of someday replanting the park with buffalo grass or tall fescue, a grass that is as attractive as traditional lawn grasses but uses 40 percent less water. The wildlife biologist agreed with these ideas. She added that the combination of groomed and wild habitats would provide areas for both humans and wildlife. In addition, she noted that creating better wildlife habitat would increase the opportunities for people to see animals. She offered to select the trees and shrubs that would be most appealing to wildlife as well as compatible with a park environment.

The aquatic ecologist recommended establishing a marsh at the far end of the pond. He pointed out that cattails and other marsh plants would provide good habitat for fish. He also said that the marsh would serve as breeding grounds for the insects that fish, frogs, bats, and many species of birds eat. The wildlife biologist added that the plants associated with the marsh would provide food and shelter for many species of mammals and birds.

The urban planner also liked the idea of a marsh. She discussed the values of marshes and other *wetlands* in urban areas. Wetland is a general term used to describe land that is soggy or covered by water all or part of the year. She also mentioned the possibility of linking the park to other habitats by a natural corridor along the nearby stream.

The parks supervisor reminded the other committee members that large,

Cattails

grassy areas needed to be preserved for soccer and volleyball games. They agreed with her and planned to set aside ample room for recreation fields. The supervisor also suggested the possibility of offering guided wildlife walks in the park on Saturday mornings. Lastly, the committee set tentative dates for public meetings at which the local residents would be able to express their desires and concerns and make recommendations for the park plan.

❖ The Benefits of Urban Planning and Wildlife Management

Years later this park is an inviting place for both wildlife and humans. There are groomed lawns where people can play sports and shade trees under which they can rest. There are picnic tables and a pond full of fish. And as the committee had hoped, there are many opportunities to watch wildlife. Most of these opportunities were brought about by improvements to the habitat. *Wildlife management* refers to efforts, including habitat improvement, that enhance conditions for wildlife populations or communities. Wildlife management also pertains to efforts to control wild animals so that they do not become a nuisance to humans or, for some species, so that they do not become overcrowded and destroy their own habitat.

Now that the trees in the park have grown larger, fox squirrels, flickers, crows, and great horned owls have taken up residence there. In cities, as in natural environments, these species require mature trees where they can nest, perch, and find food. Fox squirrels spend most of their time

Fox Squirrel

Fox
Squirrel

in old trees. During the fall they race up and down tree trunks, gathering seeds and nuts from the branches and burying them in the ground. Every now and then squirrels will stop to eat what they're gathering. The squirrel coming down the tree in the picture has a mouthful of elm seeds. Fox squirrels can nibble the edges and tear away the seed coats of tiny elm seeds faster than you can count to ten.

The seeds and nuts that squirrels bury in fall are retrieved in winter when food is not readily available. The cool earth keeps them fresh—almost like storing food in a freezer. And forgotten seeds and nuts are sometimes tomorrow's trees! Like the blue jay, fox squirrels are native to the hardwood forests of the eastern United States. They were introduced into Colorado in the early 1900s.

Next time you visit your neighborhood park listen for a loud series of "wick, wick, wick, wick" calls. Then watch for a flash of orange and a show of white. That's a northern flicker. Flickers are a type of woodpecker. Like most woodpeckers they look like they're riding a roller coaster when they fly—up, down, up, down. As they fly from tree to tree, it's easy to see the bright orange undersides of their wings and the white patch on their rump. Parks are excellent urban habitats for flickers because they have similar traits to a flicker's natural habitat. In the wild, flickers require open forests or sparsely-wooded areas where the ground is clear of thick vegetation or brush.

Flicker

Flickers need mature trees in which to build their nests. Their nests are made of a bed of wood chips in the bottom of a deep tree cavity. After the male selects the site, he and the female excavate the cavity by chipping away at the wood with their powerful beaks. Excavating can take up to two weeks and the holes may be from nine inches to three feet deep. Woodpeckers are adapted to pecking wood. They have sturdy beaks and thick skulls that can withstand the constant pounding. They also have strong claws and rigid tail feathers that enable them to cling to tree trunks while they work. The cavities they excavate are popular with other nesting birds, too. During the 1950s two scientists recorded a decline in Colorado's flicker population. Their study concluded that starlings, a recent arrival to Colorado, were competing with flickers for nest holes.

Don't always look for flickers in trees or even in flight. Often you will find these large birds on the ground, probing for insects in the grass and at the base of trees. Most of the time they are looking for ants. Flickers eat more ants than any other bird in North America. However, they also dine on beetles, crickets, grasshoppers, caterpillars, and other insects. In the late fall and winter they eat wild berries and seeds, as well as the suet at your feeder.

Another interesting bird that often resides in Front Range parks is the great horned owl. In the evening you may have heard the six-noted hoot of the great horned owl. It sounds something like "whoo! whoo-whoo-whoo! whoo! whoo!" During the day these owls usually perch quietly in trees close to the trunks or

*Northern
Flicker*

well-hidden among the leaves. Great horned owls are large, powerful birds that have few, if any, predators. However, as you can tell from the picture, they are subject to harassment. If crows, blue jays, and other birds see a great horned owl they are likely to mob it. They flock together around the owl, dive, and sometimes peck at it in an attempt to scare it away. Sometimes they succeed. If so, you may have the rare chance of watching a great horned owl fly during the day—with a mob of angry, squawking birds chasing it.

Why do crows and jays mob great horned owls? Most likely because they are threatened by their presence. Owls are excellent hunters—quiet, swift, and precise. Although great horned owls mainly eat cottontails, they don't hesitate to pluck crows or jays right off of their night roosts. Their diet is extremely varied; almost everything on this park's "menu" would satisfy their appetite. They eat muskrats, Canada geese, mallards, fox squirrels, and even skunks! Occasionally, they strike the large stick and leaf nests of fox squirrels. When frightened squirrels flee the nest, the owls seize them with their talons.

Great horned owls usually have a regular roost site where they eat their prey. These sites may be old nests or fallen logs. Beneath them you can find regurgitated *pellets* of undigestible hair, feathers, and bones. Pulling pellets apart is an excellent way to find out what the owls in your area are eating. It's always a good idea to wear rubber gloves when investigating pellets.

*Great
Horned
Owl
& Crows*

Crow

108   One of the most adaptable birds is the crow. Crows are found throughout the United States and do well wherever humans have altered the land. They are also one of the most intelligent birds. Crows mimic the sounds of other animals, including the human voice, and they have a relatively complex language. In fact, scientists have interpreted twenty-three different crow calls. One is the assembly call. This "cawrr...cawrr...cawrr... cawrr" sound is given when a crow sees a great horned owl or other predator. Other crows respond to the assembly call by flocking together to help mob the predator. Another call is given when a crow is in immediate danger. This dispersal call warns other crows to fly away. Perhaps crows give this call when they see a great horned owl fly near their roost site, or when people climb up their nest trees.

Can crows count? Some scientists think so. Their studies suggest that crows identify each other by the number of cawrr sounds they make and whether the cawrrs, and the time between each cawrr, is long or short. In the fall and winter when crows flock, having names helps to keep the flock members together. Usually crows identify themselves with one to six cawrrs, but they can use as many as nine. If you were a crow your name might be "cawrr-cawrr-cawrr-cawrr" or "cawrr—cawrr" or simply "caaaawrr."

After the crow in the picture swallows the berry in its beak, it might strut over and snatch up the wolf spider crawling up the base of the tree. Aside from being another animal's dinner, wolf spiders, as well as other spiders, play

Wolf Spider

important roles in the ecosystem. They help to control insect populations in cities and elsewhere because insects are their chief food items. Unlike spiders that spin webs or lie-in-wait in their burrows, wolf spiders chase and catch their prey. They seek safety and rest in silk-lined burrows. When wolf spiders build their burrows, they bind up the loose soil in tiny silk pouches and carry it away.

Muskrat

❖ Carrying Capacity

Whenever biologists suggest making improvements to increase the number of animals living in a habitat, they are referring to the concept of *carrying capacity*. Carrying capacity is the number of animals, sometimes including humans, that a habitat can sustain. For example, before any of the planning committee's suggestions were enacted, there weren't any crows living in city park. After the first trees planted grew tall, some crows moved into the park, attracted by the sturdy nest and perch sites of mature trees. As more trees were planted and grew, more crows moved in. The marsh also attracted crows. Crows eat snails, snakes, frogs, and salamanders, which are common in marshes. In the fall and winter they eat berries and fruit. After the berry bushes were planted, crow numbers may have increased even more.

This park's ability to support a growing crow population illustrates that a habitat's carrying capacity is flexible. Carrying capacities vary over time depending on the condition of the habitat, the availability and abundance of food, water, shelter, and space.

Animal populations are also *dynamic,* or likely to change. As illustrated by the crows, population size changes as the habitat condition changes. Population size also varies with the seasons. For some species, populations fluctuate over a period of years. For example, muskrat populations cycle every ten to fourteen years, at least in parts of their range.

Cycles are repeated fluctuations in population numbers. For muskrats, the general pattern is as follows: a period of low muskrat numbers, followed by a period of high population, followed by starvation and a massive muskrat die-off. This pattern may not be as pronounced or occur at all in urban areas where muskrats and their habitat are scarce.

Muskrats have fascinated scientists for years and many studies have been done to learn more about them. One study concludes that the number of muskrats in a marsh depends more on the length of the shoreline than on the size of the pond or lake. In other words, more muskrats can live in ponds with an irregular shoreline than in ponds without one. The pond in this picture could probably support a higher population of muskrats if it were less round and had more little coves.

Muskrats are mainly nocturnal, but it is not uncommon to see them out during the day. Like their beaver relatives, muskrats build either dens in river banks or lodges in marshy ponds. However, instead of building lodges out of tree trunks and branches like beavers do, muskrats use cattail stems and roots, as well as other aquatic plants.

Muskrats eat many things, but their most important foods are bulrushes and cattails. Not only do they eat the leaves and stems of these and other aquatic plants, they also dig up the roots. Roots bind marsh soils together.

During periods of high muskrat populations, it is this digging that can destroy marsh habitat. On the other hand, when muskrat numbers are not high, root digging may be beneficial to other species of wildlife. For example, the muskrat's digging may open up dense stands of aquatic vegetation for geese and ducks.

❖ **The Values of Wetlands**

Marshes and other types of wetlands are extremely valuable to wildlife. They provide breeding grounds for a remarkable variety of insects, fish, amphibians, reptiles, small mammals, and birds. They are also important feeding and resting areas for migrating geese and ducks. Wetlands are considered critical habitat because of their immense value to wildlife, yet many are being destroyed. Less than one-half of the original wetlands of the lower forty-eight states remain. The same is true for Colorado; it is estimated that only forty-four percent of Colorado's original wetlands still exist. Most of the original wetlands were drained and filled for agricultural and urban development. To ensure the survival of many species, the remaining wetlands must be preserved and others restored.

During the fall and spring great flocks of Canada geese migrate through Colorado. There is also a large population of geese that resides here throughout the year. Canada geese are dependent on wetlands, especially shallow open water where they find abundant food and

Canada Goose

safety from predators. Like ducks, they tip bottom up to feed on roots, leaves, and seeds at the bottom of ponds and rivers. The geese in this picture have found ideal habitat: open water, marsh, and lawn grasses. Part of the reason that Canada geese are so common in parks and on golf courses is because the grass in these groomed areas is fertilized and very nutritious. The other reason is that the vegetation on parks and golf courses is relatively sparse. Canada geese are wary of predators and do not flock to areas with dense vegetation.

Wetlands are valuable to people as well. Some types can reduce the impacts of floods by absorbing vast quantities of water that would otherwise flood developed areas. They also act as buffers that prevent the erosion of shorelines and riverbanks. Wetland plants can purify water by taking up and using fertilizer pollutants, especially nitrogen and phosphorous, that run off of lawns and agricultural lands. They can also filter harmful petroleum products from street runoff. In addition, wetlands are ideal places to bird watch, study nature, and go fishing.

❖ **Open Space**

The most recent development in this park's management has been the acquisition of *open space* land next to the park. Open space is a term used to describe undeveloped public lands that are left in their natural state. Typically, these lands are within city limits or

Human Being & Dog

just beyond the border. The open space this city acquired is in the form of a riparian corridor. It connects the park to other parks and natural areas throughout the city and beyond.

Parks and open space lands are excellent places for humans to mingle with wildlife. When the two habitat types are side by side the opportunities for wildlife watching may be even greater. Some animals are more likely to use groomed parks if natural areas are close by. For example, striped skunks and raccoons may venture into a park every now and then as long as the protection of brushy vegetation is nearby. Skunks typically like tall grasses and shrubby areas, edges of woodlots, and wooded areas near water where they sleep in burrows or hollow logs. The open space land on the far side of the pond provides ideal skunk habitat.

Striped Skunk

You are probably keenly aware of the skunk's best defense—its awful smelling spray. When frightened by a predator, up goes its tail and out comes a smelly oil. Like a nozzle on a garden hose, the skunk can release a direct stream or a fine mist. It is a short-range marksman, accurate only up to eight feet. One of its most common targets is free-roaming dogs that haven't learned that skunks are better left alone. It is always a good idea to keep dogs tightly leashed in parks to protect them from skunks, but especially so that they do not disturb wildlife.

Striped skunks are interesting animals to observe. During the early morning and evening, you may see them digging small holes in the ground. They are

Tiger Salamander

in search of insects or small mammals in underground burrows. If you watch a skunk long enough you may see movements that remind you of a hungry cat. Like a cat, it may lie-in-wait with its eyes firmly fixed to the ground just ahead, then stalk very slowly and pounce. Usually their prey is a grasshopper or a beetle, but skunks have been known to eat spiders, mice, earthworms, bees, and even tiger salamanders. Throughout the year they also feed on carrion. In fall when the insects are less plentiful, skunks eat berries and other fruits.

❖ Conclusion

In comparison to other areas in cities, parks are some of the least developed lands. With creative planning, they can be transformed into havens for urban wildlife. For most people the presence of wildlife increases the value of parks. Wildlife watching opportunities enhance the recreational, educational, and aesthetic experiences of children and adults alike. Park and recreation offices in some cities may take on the task of improving wildlife habitat in parks. If not, perhaps youth clubs, and civic and conservation organizations in your city could assist in making the improvements. Talking with the appropriate city government officials and wildlife experts is a good place to start.

Mallard

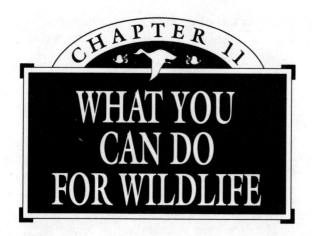

CHAPTER 11

WHAT YOU CAN DO FOR WILDLIFE

*P*lanning and managing habitats for urban wildlife go hand in hand. These efforts are especially important in urban areas because of the conflicting demands on land.

In the previous chapter, a team of professional biologists and planners took responsibility for improving a park's habitat for both wildlife and people. Planning teams are very important. However, you don't need to leave habitat planning and management up to the professionals. Alone or with others, you can play an important role in preserving, restoring, and even creating wildlife habitat in your city or suburb. Opportunities include undertaking projects in your own backyard or school yard, and promoting neighborhood or city-wide efforts.

Whether you own a balcony on a high-rise building, a small suburban lot, or three acres on the outskirts of town, there are ways you can create or improve wildlife habitat.

Consider a five-by-eight-foot balcony. With little effort and expense, you can create a haven for birds, butterflies, and maybe even for fox squirrels. Balcony habitats generally consist of potted plants, flower boxes or hanging baskets, trellises with spreading vines, suspended water baths, and bird and squirrel feeders.

Here are a few tips for creating high-rise habitats. Plan your space and make sure your balcony will support the added weight.

Tiger
Swallowtail

Consider wind and other weather factors. Provide a combination of habitat components for the species you want to attract. If you can not provide each species with all of its habitat needs, do not worry. It's likely that the local habitat will. To ensure long summers of butterfly viewing, select plants that will bloom one after the other throughout the growing season. Zinnias and impatiens work well in flower boxes, as do clematis and honeysuckle vine on a trellis. Planting milkweed in pots will attract monarchs and tiger swallowtails. If you would like to feed yourself as well as the butterflies, consider growing parsley, peppermint, dill, and carrots.

Birds will probably be your most frequent visitors. As suggested in the winter backyard chapter, provide different types of seeds to attract a diversity of species. If mature trees are nearby, your balcony may also become the local diner for fox squirrels. Sprinkling cracked corn or striped sunflower seeds on the floor or railing is an inexpensive way to lure squirrels

away from your bird feeders. Water is essential.
You may want to hang a bird bath or attach a
dish of water to the balcony railing. Of course,
keeping the cats indoors will improve your
chances of attracting wildlife.

Many of the tips discussed above would also
apply to a small suburban or urban lot.
However, with an actual piece of land there is
much more you can do to enhance the habitat,
and many more species you can attract. Some
examples of habitat improvements are provided
in the summer backyard chapter. Another way
to provide habitat is to *xeriscape* your yard.
Xeriscaping is the practice of landscaping with
plants that are adapted to *xeric,* or dry, lands.
By doing so, many Front Range urbanites are
creating habitat similar to the native prairie
right in the middle of the city. If enough people were to xeriscape at least half of their yards,
a lot of water would be saved and native habitat restored.

Creating pools of water will also improve
wildlife habitat on either small or large parcels
of land. Shallow pools attract songbirds,
amphibians, insects, and the occasional garter
snake. To construct a pool, use a piece of rope
to choose a pleasing shape. Once you have
selected the location, dig the pool so that the
sides gently slope to a deeper center. Layer the
depression with sand, wire mesh, and concrete
to prevent the water from leaking out. The
sides of the pool should be as shallow as one-
half inch and the center no deeper than four
inches. Then, fill the hole with water and place
a big rock in the center to create a small island.
Afterwards, sit back and watch birds bathe in
the shallows and alight on the rock to sip
water.

Ponds and wetlands involve considerably more expense and effort to create and maintain than pools. However, if constructed properly they can provide habitat for many wetland species. Some Front Range educators and students have created wetlands on school grounds to enhance habitat for wildlife, as well as to build their own living laboratories. They consulted with experts in wetland creation or restoration before choosing a site, designing the shape, and selecting wetland vegetation.

Bird in Pool

Building brush and rock piles are simple, inexpensive ways to create cover. Inside these structures wildlife find insect prey, rear their young, and seek protection from predators and harsh weather. Some of the more common brush and rock pile visitors are small mammals, reptiles, amphibians, insects, and birds. In general, brush piles consist of a base of crisscrossed logs and a covering of broken tree limbs and sticks. Placing the broken limbs upside down creates a tangle of twigs around the base of the brush pile through which small animals can scurry. Once inside, they can rest in the spaces between the crisscrossed logs.

Rock piles should be built with an assortment of big and small rocks. In the winter, if the spaces between the rocks are large enough, they offer cottontails shelter from the snow and wind. Rock piles are especially good summer homes for cold-blooded animals like lizards and snakes. They provide warm rocks for basking in the early morning sunshine and cool inner spaces to hide from the midday heat. They also provide homes for slugs, worms, and insects.

One way that students can improve conditions for wildlife in their cities is to improve habitat in their school yards. You and other students could make a big contribution to your school community by designing and landscaping a wildlife sanctuary. To ensure that you have a workable design and the support of your school, you should request the help of biology teachers, school administrators, and perhaps the Parent Teacher Association. In addition, the Colorado Division of Wildlife (CDOW) has a school yard habitat improvement program for just this kind of project. The program provides qualified applicants with money to purchase native vegetation for their school yards. To qualify, students must come up with a workable landscape design for wildlife habitat. For more information on this program contact the CDOW Project Wild office. The address appears on page vii.

As an urban resident, you can promote city- and county-wide efforts to identify, protect, and improve habitats within and around your city. For example, in the previous chapter, citizens made it known to city officials that they wanted more wildlife viewing opportunities. Had they not done so, the park and open space may never have become the wildlife havens they are today.

The possibilities for creative planning are endless. In some cities, progressive planners and biologists are identifying valuable, unique, and rare habitats within and on the outskirts of cities, wherever development is likely to occur. They are also purchasing natural areas and creating habitats so that all citizens

Rock Pile

are within reasonable walking distance of a park, wetland, stream corridor, or other wildlife habitat. Organizations such as the National Institute for Urban Wildlife and the National Wildlife Federation will certify residential yards, school grounds, and entire cities as wildlife sanctuaries. The requirement for sanctuary status is the enhancement or creation of wildlife. Please see page viii for addresses.

Some agencies and conservation organizations are promoting environmental education programs to help create a more lasting and meaningful experience for those who visit urban natural areas. Environmental educators know that the values of these natural areas extend far beyond city limits and that citizens who understand urban wildlife have a better appreciation for wildlife in general.

Creating, enhancing, restoring, and preserving habitat in cities have obvious benefits for urban wildlife. With habitat, wild animals can survive in urban areas. With high quality habitat, urban populations of wild animals can be large and healthy. You might wonder, though, whether people, through their enjoyment of seeing wild animals everyday, are the ones who benefit the most from sharing cities with wildlife.

*House
Finch*

SUGGESTED READINGS

Adams, L.W. and L.E. Dove. 1989. Wildlife reserves and corridors in the urban environment: a guide to ecological landscape planning and resource conservation. Columbia, Maryland: National Institute for Urban Wildlife.

___, 1984. Urban wetlands for stormwater control and wildlife enhancement. Columbia, Maryland: National Institute for Urban Wildlife.

Busch, P.S. 1970. City lots: living things in vacant spots. New York: World Publishing Company.

Cooper, A., A. Armstrong and C. Kampert. 1990. The wildwatch book. Niwot, Colorado: Robert Rinehart Publishers.

Dove, L.E. 1983. Urban wildlife manager's notebook series. Columbia, Maryland: National Institute for Urban Wildlife.

Harrison, G. H. 1979. The backyard bird watcher. New York: Simon and Schuster.

Heberman, Ethan. 1989. The city kid's field guide. New York: Simon and Schuster.

Huddleston, S. and M. Hussey. 1981. Grow native: landscaping with native and apt plants of the Rocky Mountains. Denver: Huddleston and Hussey.

Kress, S.W. 1985. The Audubon Society guide to attracting birds. New York: Charles Scribner's Sons.

SUGGESTED
READINGS

Leedy, D.L. and L.W. Adams. 1984. A guide to urban wildlife management. Columbia, Maryland: National Institute for Urban Wildlife.

___, R.M. Maestro and T.M. Franklin. 1978. Planning for wildlife in cities and suburbs. Washington, DC: Office of Biological Services, Fish and Wildlife Service, U.S. Dept. of Interior, and Chicago: American Society of Planning Officials.

Loeffler, C. 1990. Taking a look at urban wildlife. Colorado Springs: Colorado Division of Wildlife.

Rinehart, F.R. and E.A. Webb, editors. 1990. Close to home: Colorado's Urban Wildlife. Niwot, Colorado: Roberts Rinehart Publishers.

Tufts, C. 1988. The Backyard Naturalist. Washington, D.C.: National Wildlife Federation.

)

GLOSSARY

adaptation - behavior or characteristic that helps an organism survive in its environment

amphibians - cold-blooded vertebrates, such as frogs and salamanders, that spend part of their lives in water and part on land

behavioral adaptation - ways that animals behave to help them survive in a particular environment

biodiversity - diversity of native species, the genetic diversity within each species, and the diversity of ecological processes within ecosystems

browse - to selectively eat the nutritious branch tips of shrubs and trees, the way that deer and other hoofed mammals forage

cache - store in a hidden place

carnivores - animals that eat animals

carrion - rotting flesh of a dead animal

carrying capacity - number of animals (sometimes including humans) that a habitat can sustain

cavity - nest hole in a tree

community - group of organisms that live together in an ecosystem

composition - the make-up of a community or the species living in a particular area

competition - interaction that occurs between organisms when shared resources are in limited supply

consumers - animals and some plants that live

off of the organic matter of other organisms

corridors - strips of land that differ from the habitats surrounding them

cycles - repeated fluctuations in animal population numbers

diapause - physiological adaptation of insects to cold weather, similar to hibernation

dispersal - process usually occurring in the late summer or fall in which many young animals leave their parents' home ranges to establish their own

diversity - variety

dynamic - likely to change, unstable

ecological niche - role that a species plays in an ecosystem

ecology - scientific study of how living things interact with each other and their environment

ecosystems functioning groups of living and non-living things in a particular environment

erosion - the gradual wearing away of land surface by wind, water, ice, or other natural forces

exotics - another term for nonnative species

exploit - use resources efficiently or intensively

exploitative competition - an indirect form of competition, in which one species uses a common resource more efficiently and intensively than the other, leaving too little for the other to survive in the range where the species overlap

farm colonies - planned communities along the Front Range where members paid dues and worked together to build irrigation systems

fledglings - birds just learning to fly

food chain - transfer of energy from one organism to the next by foraging or predation, each organism is analogous to a link in a chain

forbs - leafy, non-woody plants

Front Range - a large geographic area where the eastern edge of the Rocky Mountains meets the western edge of the Great Plains. Commonly refs to a 150-mile urban corridor tht extends from Fort Collins to Pueblo, Colorado

gene flow - "movement" of genes through a population as a result of reproduction

generalists - species whose survival needs are not specific and who can change their behavior to take advantage of new opportunities

genes - hereditary material passed from parent to offspring

global - of a worldly nature

habitat components - the environmental factors, such as food, water, shelter, and space, that make up an organism's habitat

habitat fragmentation - process by which large habitat types are broken into pieces, often resulting in habitat fragments too small or inadequate to accommodate the previously occurring species

habitat islands - isolated habitat patches without connecting corridors

habitat requirement - environmental factors, such as food, water, shelter, and space, that an animal needs to survive in a particular area

heat islands - a term for cities to describe their higher average temperature

herbivores - animals that eat plants

hibernation - long-term condition during which body temperatures drop and heart and breathing rates slow down, a physiological adaptation of some animals that helps them cope with cold weather

home range - smallest area in which an animal finds adequate food, water, shelter, and space

hypothesis - a possible explanation of a behavior or trait that can be tested scientifically

immigration - movement of an animal or plant into a recipient patch from a source patch

insectivores - animals that eat insects

interdependence - two (or more) organisms that

are somewhat, if not totally, dependent on each other for their ability to function

interference competition - when a more aggressive species drives competing species away from a common resource

kit - term for baby beaver or rabbit

larvae - immature feeding form of an insect that hatches from an egg

limiting factor - a habitat component that is in short supply

migration - natural movement of animals from one place to another for breeding or feeding purposes

molt - process of birds dropping old feathers and growing new ones

native species - species that naturally occur in a particular area

natural history - non-scientific study of animal and plant life and the natural environment

nocturnal - active at night

non-native species - species that do not naturally occur in their present location

omnivores - animals that during any one season or the course of a year eat both plants and animals (including insects)

open space - undeveloped public lands that are left in a natural state

pellets - balls of undigestible hair, feathers, and bones that birds of prey regurgitate after eating prey

pests - animals or plants that for various reasons cause real or perceived problems for humans

physiological adaptations - ways that an animal's body prepares for certain environmental conditions

plains - an extensive area of flat or rolling treeless country

plumage - covering of feathers

population - group of individuals of one species

prairie - life zone where grasses are dominant and few trees exist

producers - organisms that make food

rabies - rare but serious disease that is transmissible to humans by some mammals

raptors - "birds of prey," birds such as hawks, owls, eagles, and shrikes that kill their prey, usually fish, reptiles, and small mammals

recipient area - small habitat fragment, often inside city limits, that alone may be too small to permit adequate gene flow to ensure the survival of wildlife populations there

resource - a component of the environment that a plant or animal can use

riparian corridors - rivers together with the lands that border them

rookery - place where birds of the same species nest together

scientific method - process of asking questions, formulating hypotheses, making and testing predictions about the possible answers, and eventually coming up with answers that either support or fail to support the hypothesis

settlement patterns - the way in which people settle on the land, usually either loosely clustered in small towns, tightly custered in big cities, or scattered across the land on farms

source area - land that is in good condition and large enough to sustain an adequate gene flow for the wildlife populations that live there

spawn - to produce or deposit eggs (used for aquatic animals, especially fish)

specialists - species whose survival needs and adaptations are specific to a particular ecosystem and have evolved with the ecosystem for thousands or millions of years

species - group of organisms that do or could interbreed and are reproductively isolated from all other such groups and have viable offspring

suet - soft chunks of animal fat

theories - scientific hypotheses or ideas that have not been falsified after many rigorous experiments, "tried and true" ideas

torpor - short-term condition during which body temperatures drop and heart and breathing rates slow down, a physiological adaptation that helps some animals cope with cold weather

tropical deforestation - process of cutting and/or burning rain forests and brushlands in the tropics that results in short-term economic benefits, but long-term environmental tragedies including habitat fragmentation and global warming

urban wildlife - wild animals (and plants) that have adjusted to living in city environments

web of life - web of connections between living and non-living elements in the natural world; illustrates the interdependence of nature

wetland - general term used to describe land that is soggy or covered by water all or part of the year

wildlife management - professional discipline based on scientific research that pertains to efforts that enhance conditions for wildlife populations or communities, or that control wildlife populations to prevent them from becoming pests

xeric - arid or dry

xeriscaping - practice of landscaping with plants that are adapted to dry lands

yearlings - last year's young

zoning laws - laws that control what and where you can build

INDEX

omnivore 59, 60
open space 13, 93, 112, 113,
    121
owls 38, 51, 107
    barn 26, 27
    burrowing 35
    great horned **98-99**, 104,
    106, **107**, 108

pellets 107
pest 11, 41, 43, 44
physiological adaptation 69
pigeon 11, 12, **30-31**, 38, 41,
    42, 43, **44**
plains garter snake 8, **46-47**,
    53, 59, **60**, 119
plumage 36
pocket gopher 11, **12**
populations (ecological) 19,
    52, 70, 74, 90, 91, 92, 93,
    104, 109, 110, 122
prairie dog 9, 12, 28, **29**, **30-
    31**, **35**, 36, 42, 50, **90**, 91
prairie 21, 28, 35, 39, 82, 91,
    96, 119
producer 59

rabies 11
raccoon 11, **46-47**, **50**, 51,
    60, 70, 113
raptor 38
recipient area **92**, 93
riparian corridors 55, 82, 93,
    96, 103, 122
robin See American robin
rookery 95

scientific method 27
settlement pattern 18
skunk See striped skunk
source area **92**, 93

spawn 85
specialist 34, 35, 42, 50, 56
species 2
starling 11, 12, **30-31**, 38,
    40, 41, 43, **56**, 57, 70, 106
striped skunk 11, **98-99**, 102,
    107, **113**, 114
suet 67, 73, 74, 76, 106

theories 26, 37
tiger swallowtail butterfly **46-
    47**, 53, 60, **118**
tiger salamander **98-99**, 109,
    113, 114
torpor 69
tropical deforestation 90

urban wildlife 1

web of life 58, 59, 60
western meadowlark **30-31**,
    36, 39, 42
wetlands 103, 111, 112, 120,
    122
white sucker **78-79**, 84, **85**,
    86, 87
white-breasted nuthatch **62-
    63**, 67, 68, 69, 71
white-footed mouse 30-31,
    38, 39
wildlife management 104, 119
wolf spider **98-99**, **108**, 109

xeric 119
xeriscape 119

yearling 83
yellow warbler **46-47**, **54**, 58,
    59, 67

zoning laws **40**

FIELD NOTES

FIELD NOTES

FIELD NOTES